Contents

How to Eat Gluten-Free and Love it

What Is Gluten Anyway?

Gluten is a protein that is found in wheat, rye and barley. There are many reasons people avoid gluten. Celiac disease is the most serious. There are others who have a sensitivity to gluten and just feel better when they avoid it. Some people are allergic to wheat itself. You know which category you belong in if you're reading this book!

No More Bread? No Pasta?

At first, going gluten-free may sound awfully limiting. Fortunately, there are many more delicious foods on the gluten-free list than the forbidden list. There are also more and more products, from cereals to baking mixes to pastas, that are now being formulated in gluten-free versions. These days you'll find them not just in health food stores and online, but also on the shelves of most major supermarkets.

Some Good News

Spotting hidden gluten in processed foods is a lot easier now thanks to the FDA's Food Allergy Labeling Law that went into effect in 2004. Since wheat is a common allergen, any product that contains wheat or is derived from it must say so on the label. That means formerly questionable ingredients, such as modified food starch or maltodextrin, must now show wheat as part of their name if they were made from it (for example, "wheat maltodextrin"). Be aware that this ONLY applies to foods produced in the U.S. and Canada. Imports are a different matter.

More Good News

Look at your dietary restrictions as an opportunity to try new foods. Add quinoa and chickpea flour to your cupboard. Use corn tortillas to make sandwiches or lasagna. You'll find easy recipes in this book that are so delicious you'll forget that they're gluten-free. Healthy eating may actually be easier without gluten, too. Adding more fresh produce to your meals, eating less processed food and avoiding refined flour are all steps to a better diet for anyone.

The Short List

Sensitivities differ from person to person and ingredients differ from brand to brand. Always check the label's fine print. This is an abbreviated list of some common foods.

•Red Lights• (contain gluten)	•Yellow Lights• (check ingredients)	•Green Lights• (no gluten)
barley	baking powder	beans
beer	barbecue sauce	buckwheat
bran	emulsifiers	cellophane noodles (bean thread noodles)
brewer's yeast	flavorings	
bulgur	frozen vegetables with sauce	chickpea flour (garbanzo flour)
cereal	marinades	corn, cornmeal
commercial baked goods	mustard	dairy
couscous	nondairy creamer	eggs
durum	oats*	fruit
graham	pasta sauce	lentils
gravies and sauces	salad dressings	meat and poultry
imitation seafood	soy sauce**	millet
kamut	vegetable broth	nuts
malt, malt flavoring and malt vinegar		potatoes
matzo	*Most oats are processed in facilities that also handle wheat products. Look for oats processed in a dedicated gluten-free facility.	quinoa
orzo		rice, rice flour
pizza	**Most soy sauce is brewed from soybeans and wheat. Look for brands that skip the brewing process and use soy concentrate and caramel coloring instead.	rice noodles
pretzels		seafood
rye		soy, soy flour
seitan		tapioca
semolina		tofu
spelt		vegetables (fresh, canned or frozen without sauce)
wheat		

Supermarket Savvy

Before you rush off to buy a cupboard full of specialty products, remember that most basic ingredients are naturally gluten-free. You can pick up fresh produce, meat or fish without worrying. However, frozen dinners and fish sticks are no longer on your list. This doesn't mean you can't have your favorite foods anymore. It just means you will be making some adjustments.

Impulse shopping isn't a great option either. Most supermarkets stock huge displays with brightly colored boxes of highly processed, gluten-filled items. It may also amaze you how many aisles you can skip when you no longer wander aimlessly amidst the latest bread, cracker and snack items.

Of course, you will want to stock up on certain things so that you're prepared to eat well on your new diet. Five years ago a health food store was the only place to buy specialty flours and mixes. Fortunately, today most supermarkets offer just about everything you need.

The Gluten-Free Pantry

Cooking gluten-free is easier if you keep these staples on hand.

- ❑ beans and lentils
- ❑ chickpea flour
- ❑ corn grits
- ❑ cornmeal and cornstarch
- ❑ corn tortillas and taco shells
- ❑ GF cereal (corn and/or rice)
- ❑ GF flour blends (page 5)
- ❑ GF mixes for your favorite brownies, cookies or muffins
- ❑ GF pasta in various shapes

- ❑ GF soy sauce
- ❑ polenta
- ❑ quinoa
- ❑ rice (arborio rice, basmati rice)
- ❑ rice flour (brown, white and sweet rice flour)
- ❑ rice noodles
- ❑ tapioca flour
- ❑ wild rice
- ❑ xanthan gum

Flour Blends and Friends

Why can't there be a single one-for-one substitute for wheat flour? Unfortunately wheat flour performs many different functions and is made up of both protein (the gluten) and starches. It helps make pie crust flaky, cookies chewy and breads crusty. There is no one GF flour that can recreate all those benefits, but that's no reason to give up baking. With two basic flour blends in your refrigerator you can turn out yummy cakes, cookies and even yeast breads. Both of these recipes can be doubled or tripled. For longer storage, keep flour blends in the freezer.

Gluten-Free All-Purpose Flour Blend

- 1 cup white rice flour
- 1 cup sorghum flour
- 1 cup tapioca flour
- 1 cup cornstarch
- 1 cup almond flour or coconut flour

Combine all ingredients in large bowl. Whisk to make sure flours are evenly distributed. Store in airtight container in the refrigerator.

Makes about 5 cups

Gluten-Free Flour Blend for Yeast Breads

- 1 cup brown rice flour
- 1 cup sorghum flour
- 1 cup tapioca flour
- 1 cup cornstarch
- ¾ cup millet flour*
- ⅓ cup instant mashed potato flakes

If millet flour is not available, substitute chickpea flour.

Combine all ingredients in large bowl. Whisk to make sure ingredients are evenly distributed. Store in airtight container in the refrigerator.

Makes about 5 cups

Start Smart

denver brunch bake

  2 tablespoons butter, divided
½ cup diced onion
½ cup diced green bell pepper
½ cup diced red bell pepper
½ cup cubed ham
  6 eggs
  1 cup whole milk
½ teaspoon salt
¼ teaspoon red pepper flakes
  4 slices gluten-free bread, cut into ½-inch cubes
¾ cup (3 ounces) shredded Cheddar cheese, divided

1. Grease 9-inch baking dish with 1 tablespoon butter.

2. Melt remaining 1 tablespoon butter in large skillet over medium heat. Add onion and bell peppers; cook and stir 3 minutes. Add ham; cook and stir 2 minutes.

3. Beat eggs, milk, salt and red pepper flakes in large bowl. Add bread cubes, ham mixture and ½ cup cheese; mix well. Pour into prepared dish. Cover and refrigerate 8 hours or overnight.

4. Preheat oven to 350°F. Sprinkle casserole with remaining ¼ cup cheese.

5. Bake 45 minutes to 1 hour or until knife inserted into center comes out clean.
Makes 4 servings

buttermilk pancakes

    2 cups Gluten-Free All-Purpose Flour Blend (page 5)*
 1 ½ tablespoons sugar
    1 teaspoon baking powder
    1 teaspoon baking soda
    ½ teaspoon salt
 2 ¼ cups buttermilk
    2 eggs
    2 tablespoons butter, melted and cooled
       Vegetable oil
       Maple syrup and additional butter

Or use any all-purpose gluten-free flour blend that does not contain xanthan gum.

1. Combine flour blend, sugar, baking powder, baking soda and salt in large bowl. Whisk buttermilk, eggs and 2 tablespoons butter in small bowl. Gradually whisk buttermilk mixture into flour mixture until smooth.

2. Heat oil on griddle or large nonstick skillet over medium heat. Pour ¼ cupfuls of batter 2 inches apart onto griddle. Cook 2 minutes or until lightly browned and edges begin to bubble. Turn over; cook 2 minutes or until lightly browned. Serve with maple syrup and additional butter.

Makes 4 servings

Note: If you do not plan on serving the pancakes right away, keep them warm in a 200°F oven.

chocolate cherry bread

⅔ cup plus ¼ cup warm water (110°F), divided

3 tablespoons sugar, divided

1 package (¼ ounce) active dry yeast

2 cups Gluten-Free All-Purpose Flour Blend (page 5)*

1½ teaspoons xanthan gum

½ teaspoon salt

5 tablespoons butter, melted and cooled

3 eggs, at room temperature

¾ cup dried sour cherries**

4 ounces bittersweet chocolate, chopped

*Or use any all-purpose gluten-free flour blend that does not contain xanthan gum.
**If dried sour cherries aren't available, substitute dried cranberries.

1. Spray 9×5-inch loaf pan with nonstick cooking spray. Combine ¼ cup warm water, 1 tablespoon sugar and yeast in large bowl; let stand 10 minutes or until foamy.

2. Add flour blend, remaining 2 tablespoons sugar, xanthan gum and salt to yeast mixture. Whisk butter, remaining ⅔ cup warm water and eggs in small bowl. Gradually beat into flour mixture with electric mixer at low speed until well blended. Beat at medium-high speed 3 minutes or until well blended. Add cherries and chocolate; beat at low speed just until incorporated.

3. Pour batter into prepared pan. Cover and let rise in warm place about 1 hour or until batter almost reaches top of pan.

4. Preheat oven to 350°F.

5. Bake 35 to 40 minutes or until toothpick inserted into center comes out clean. Cool in pan on wire rack 10 minutes. Remove to wire rack; cool completely.   *Makes 12 servings*

Note: This bread may fall slightly after coming out of the oven.

wild rice and pepper frittata

  1 tablespoon olive oil
  1 large shallot, minced
  1 clove garlic, minced
  1 cup chopped fresh shiitake mushroom caps
  1 large roasted red bell pepper, chopped (see Note)
  1 cup cooked wild rice
  ⅜ teaspoon salt, divided
  ¼ teaspoon black pepper, divided
  ⅛ teaspoon ground paprika
  6 eggs
  ¼ cup shredded Asiago cheese

1. Preheat broiler. Heat oil in large nonstick ovenproof skillet. Add shallot and garlic; cook and stir over medium heat 1 minute. Add mushrooms; cook and stir 5 minutes or until tender. Stir in red pepper, wild rice, ¼ teaspoon salt, ⅛ teaspoon black pepper and paprika. Cook and stir over high heat 1 minute or until liquid evaporates. Remove from heat.

2. Beat eggs in large bowl with remaining ⅛ teaspoon salt and ⅛ teaspoon black pepper. Pour eggs into skillet; tilt to spread over rice mixture. Cook over medium heat until eggs are set but still glossy. Sprinkle with cheese.

3. Broil 5 inches from heat 3 to 4 minutes or until cheese melts and edge is browned. Let stand 2 to 3 minutes. Cut into 6 wedges.

Makes 6 servings

Note: To roast a red bell pepper, broil 4 inches from heat, turning frequently with tongs to blacken all sides. Place the pepper in a paper or plastic bag, shut the bag and set it aside for 30 minutes to 1 hour to loosen the skin. Scrape off the blackened skin with a paring knife.

sour cream cranberry coffee cake

Cake

2½ cups Gluten-Free All-Purpose Flour Blend (page 5)*

2 teaspoons baking powder

1½ teaspoons xanthan gum

1 teaspoon baking soda

1 teaspoon unflavored gelatin

½ teaspoon salt

1½ cups granulated sugar

¾ cup (1½ sticks) butter, softened

3 eggs

1 cup sour cream

2 teaspoons vanilla

2 cup fresh or frozen cranberries**

Streusel

½ cup packed light brown sugar

¼ cup Gluten-Free All-Purpose Flour Blend (page 5)*

¾ teaspoon ground cinnamon

¼ teaspoon ground nutmeg

¼ teaspoon salt

3 tablespoons cold butter, cubed

*Or use any all-purpose gluten-free flour blend that does not contain xanthan gum.
**If using frozen cranberries, do not thaw before adding them to the batter as they will turn the batter red.

1. Preheat oven to 350°F. Spray 13×9-inch baking pan with nonstick cooking spray.

2. Combine 2½ cups flour blend, baking powder, xanthan gum, baking soda, gelatin and ½ teaspoon salt in medium bowl.

3. Beat granulated sugar and ¾ cup butter in large bowl with electric mixer at medium-high speed until light and fluffy. Add eggs, one at a time, beating well at medium speed after each addition. Beat in sour cream and vanilla. Add flour mixture in two additions; beat at low speed until well blended. Fold in cranberries. Pour into prepared pan.

4. Bake 40 minutes. Meanwhile for streusel, combine brown sugar, ¼ cup flour blend, cinnamon, nutmeg and ¼ teaspoon salt in small bowl. Cut in 3 tablespoons butter with pastry blender or two knives until mixture resembles coarse crumbs.

5. Sprinkle streusel evenly over coffee cake. Bake 10 minutes or until toothpick inserted into center comes out clean. Serve warm or at room temperature. *Makes 12 servings*

pumpkin muffins

2¼ cups Gluten-Free All-Purpose Flour Blend (page 5)*

½ teaspoon salt

½ teaspoon ground ginger

½ teaspoon ground nutmeg

½ teaspoon xanthan gum

¼ teaspoon baking soda

1 cup packed dark brown sugar

1 cup canned solid-pack pumpkin (not pumpkin pie filling)

½ cup (1 stick) butter, melted and cooled

2 eggs

¼ cup buttermilk

3 tablespoons molasses

1 teaspoon vanilla

*Or use any all-purpose gluten-free flour blend that does not contain xanthan gum.

1. Preheat oven to 400°F. Spray 12 standard (2½-inch) muffin cups with nonstick cooking spray.

2. Combine flour blend, salt, ginger, nutmeg, xanthan gum and baking soda in medium bowl. Whisk brown sugar, pumpkin, butter, eggs, buttermilk, molasses and vanilla in large bowl. Add flour mixture in two additions, stirring until well blended after each addition. Spoon evenly into prepared muffin cups.**

3. Bake 18 to 22 minutes or until toothpick inserted into centers comes out clean. Cool in pan 5 minutes. Remove to wire rack to cool slightly. Serve warm or at room temperature. *Makes 12 muffins*

**For best results, scoop batter into each muffin cup in a single scoop, filling to the top; do not add additional batter.*

buckwheat pancakes

1 cup buckwheat flour

2 tablespoons cornstarch

2 teaspoons baking powder

¼ teaspoon salt

¼ teaspoon ground cinnamon

1 cup milk

1 egg

2 tablespoons butter, melted, plus additional for cooking

2 tablespoons maple syrup, plus additional for serving

½ teaspoon vanilla

1. Whisk buckwheat flour, cornstarch, baking powder, salt and cinnamon in medium bowl. Combine milk, egg, 2 tablespoons butter, 2 tablespoons maple syrup and vanilla in small bowl. Whisk into dry ingredients just until combined. Let stand 5 minutes. (Batter will be thick and elastic.)

2. Brush additional butter on griddle or heat in large nonstick skillet over medium heat. Pour ¼ cupfuls of batter 2 inches apart onto griddle. Cook 2 minutes or until lightly browned and edges begin to bubble. Turn over; cook 2 minutes or until lightly browned. Serve with additional maple syrup. *Makes 4 servings*

Variation: Add ½ cup blueberries to the batter.

bacon-cheese grits

2 cups milk

½ cup quick-cooking grits

1 ½ cups (6 ounces) shredded sharp Cheddar cheese or 6 slices
    American cheese, torn into bite-size pieces

2 tablespoons butter

1 teaspoon Worcestershire sauce

½ teaspoon salt

⅛ teaspoon ground red pepper (optional)

4 thick-cut slices bacon, crisp-cooked and chopped

1. Bring milk to a boil in large saucepan over medium-high heat. Slowly stir in grits. Return to a boil. Reduce heat; cover and simmer 5 minutes, stirring frequently.

2. Remove from heat. Stir in cheese, butter, Worcestershire sauce, salt and red pepper, if desired. Cover; let stand 2 minutes or until cheese is melted. Top each serving with bacon.   *Makes 4 servings*

Variation: For a thinner consistency, add an additional ½ cup milk.

Dinner's Ready

feta and spinach stuffed turkey burgers

¼ cup gluten-free cornflake crumbs

¼ cup sliced green onions

1 egg, beaten

1 pound ground turkey

½ (10-ounce) package frozen chopped spinach, thawed and squeezed dry

⅓ cup crumbled feta cheese

¼ cup chopped black olives

¼ teaspoon black pepper

½ cup chopped fresh tomato

1. Prepare grill for direct cooking. Oil grid.

2. Combine cornflake crumbs, green onions and egg in medium bowl. Add ground turkey; mix well. Pat turkey mixture into 8 (⅜-inch-thick) patties on sheet of waxed paper.

3. Combine spinach, feta cheese, olives and pepper in small bowl. Place spinach mixture evenly on top of 4 turkey patties. Top with remaining patties; press edges to seal.

4. Grill patties over medium heat 11 to 13 minutes or until cooked through (165°F). Top with chopped tomato.   *Makes 4 servings*

spaghetti squash alfredo

4 cups cooked spaghetti squash (see Note)

½ teaspoon salt

½ teaspoon black pepper

¼ cup (½ stick) butter

1 teaspoon minced garlic

1 cup whipping cream

½ cup grated Parmesan cheese, plus additional for garnish

1 tablespoon olive oil

12 ounces (about 2 cups) frozen cooked shrimp, thawed

Chopped fresh basil (optional)

1. Sprinkle squash with salt and pepper. Melt butter in large nonstick skillet over medium-high heat. Add garlic; cook 30 seconds. Add squash; cook and stir 2 to 3 minutes or until heated through. Add cream; cook and stir 3 minutes or until sauce begins to thicken. Stir in ½ cup cheese; cook 2 minutes or until cheese is melted. Cover and keep warm.

2. Meanwhile, heat oil in large nonstick skillet over high heat. Add shrimp; cook and stir until heated through.

3. Top squash mixture with shrimp. Garnish with additional cheese and basil. *Makes 4 servings*

Note: Two medium spaghetti squash (3 to 3½ pounds) will yield about 4 cups cooked squash. To cook squash easily and quickly, pierce each squash to the center with a knife in two places. Place squash on a microwavable plate and microwave on HIGH 20 minutes. (If the microwave does not have an automatic turntable, turn squash three times during cooking.) Let stand 10 minutes. Cut off stem end and discard. Slice in half lengthwise. Scoop out seeds and center membranes and discard. Using a fork, pull squash into strands and drain in colander.

chicken kabobs over quinoa

  1 cup uncooked quinoa
  2 cups water
  1 jalapeño pepper,* seeded and finely chopped
  3 teaspoons grated lemon peel, divided
 ½ teaspoon salt, divided
  1 pound boneless skinless chicken breasts, cubed
  2 teaspoons gluten-free steak seasoning blend
  8 asparagus spears, trimmed and sliced into thirds
 16 grape tomatoes
 16 green onions, trimmed and sliced into thirds
  2 tablespoons lemon juice
  2 tablespoons extra virgin olive oil
  1 clove garlic, minced
 ¼ cup chopped cilantro

Jalapeño peppers can sting and irritate the skin, so wear rubber gloves when handling peppers and do not touch your eyes.

1. Place quinoa in fine-mesh strainer; rinse well under cold running water. Bring 2 cups water to a boil in small saucepan; stir in quinoa. Reduce heat to low; cover and simmer 10 to 15 minutes or until water is absorbed and quinoa is tender. Stir in jalapeño pepper, 2 teaspoons lemon peel and ¼ teaspoon salt. Keep warm.

2. Soak 8 (12-inch) wooden skewers 10 minutes in cold water. Sprinkle chicken with steak seasoning. Thread asparagus, chicken, tomatoes and green onions onto skewers.

3. Combine lemon juice, remaining 1 teaspoon lemon peel, oil, garlic and remaining ¼ teaspoon salt in small bowl. Reserve half of mixture; brush remaining mixture over skewers.

4. Prepare grill for direct cooking. Oil grid. Grill skewers 3 to 4 minutes on each side or until chicken is cooked through.

5. Brush skewers with reserved lemon juice mixture. Stir cilantro into quinoa; serve with skewers.   *Makes 4 servings*

spicy pork stew with roasted veggies

        1 tablespoon olive oil
    1 ½ pounds boneless pork loin, trimmed and cut into ½-inch cubes
        1 cup chopped onion
        2 red bell peppers, cut into ½-inch pieces
        8 ounces sliced mushrooms
        1 medium acorn squash, peeled and cut into ½-inch cubes
        1 can (about 14 ounces) diced tomatoes
        1 can (about 14 ounces) gluten-free chicken broth
        ½ teaspoon red pepper flakes
        ½ teaspoon black pepper
        ½ teaspoon dried thyme
            Fresh oregano (optional)

1. Heat oil in Dutch oven over medium-high heat. Add half of pork; cook about 5 minutes or until browned, stirring occasionally. Repeat with remaining pork.

2. Add onion, bell peppers and mushrooms to Dutch oven. Stir in squash, tomatoes, broth, red pepper flakes, black pepper and thyme; bring to a boil over high heat. Reduce heat; cover and simmer 1 hour or until pork is tender. Garnish with oregano.   *Makes 6 to 8 servings*

eggplant parmesan

2 egg whites

2 tablespoons water

½ cup crushed gluten-free rice cereal squares

¼ cup plus 2 tablespoons grated Parmesan cheese, divided

1 teaspoon Italian seasoning

1 large eggplant, peeled and cut into ½-inch-thick slices

2 teaspoons olive oil

1 small onion, diced

1 clove garlic, minced

2 cans (about 14 ounces each) diced tomatoes

½ teaspoon dried basil

½ teaspoon dried oregano

½ cup (2 ounces) shredded mozzarella cheese

1. Preheat oven to 350°F. Spray baking sheet with nonstick cooking spray.

2. Whisk egg whites and water in shallow dish. Combine crushed cereal, 2 tablespoons Parmesan cheese and Italian seasoning in another shallow dish. Dip eggplant slices in egg white mixture, then in cereal mixture, pressing lightly. Place in single layer in prepared pan.

3. Bake 25 to 30 minutes or until bottoms are browned. Turn slices over; bake 15 to 20 minutes or until well browned and tender.

4. Meanwhile, heat oil in medium nonstick skillet over medium-high heat. Add onion; cook and stir 5 minutes or until softened. Add garlic; cook and stir 1 minute. Stir in tomatoes, basil and oregano; bring to a boil. Reduce heat to low; simmer 15 to 20 minutes or until sauce is thickened, stirring occasionally.

5. Spray 13×9-inch baking dish with nonstick cooking spray. Spread sauce in dish. Arrange eggplant slices in single layer on top of sauce. Sprinkle with mozzarella cheese and remaining ¼ cup Parmesan cheese. Bake 15 to 20 minutes or until sauce is bubbly and cheese is melted.

Makes 4 servings

noodle-free lasagna

1 medium eggplant

2 medium zucchini

2 medium summer squash

1 ¼ pounds sweet Italian turkey sausage, casings removed

2 medium bell peppers, diced

2 cups mushrooms, thinly sliced

1 can (about 14 ounces) diced tomatoes

1 cup gluten-free tomato sauce

½ cup coarsely chopped fresh basil

1 teaspoon dried oregano

½ teaspoon salt

¼ teaspoon black pepper

1 container (15 ounces) ricotta cheese

2 cups (8 ounces) shredded mozzarella cheese

¼ cup grated Parmesan cheese

1. Preheat oven to 375°F. Cut eggplant, zucchini and yellow squash lengthwise into thin (⅛- to ¼-inch) slices. To reduce excess water, drain slices in colander (see Tip).

2. Heat large nonstick skillet over medium-high heat. Add sausage; cook 8 to 10 minutes or until cooked through, stirring to break up meat. Drain fat. Transfer to plate.

3. Add bell peppers and mushrooms to skillet; cook and stir 3 to 4 minutes or until vegetables are tender. Return sausage to skillet. Add tomatoes, tomato sauce, basil, oregano, salt and black pepper; cook and stir 1 to 2 minutes or until heated through.

4. Layer one third of eggplant, zucchini and yellow squash in 13×9-inch nonstick baking pan. Spread half of ricotta cheese over vegetables. Top with one third of tomato sauce mixture. Sprinkle evenly with half of mozzarella cheese. Repeat layers once, ending with final layer of vegetables and tomato sauce mixture. Sprinkle with Parmesan cheese; cover with foil.

5. Bake 45 minutes. Remove foil; bake 10 to 15 minutes or until vegetables are tender. Let stand 10 minutes before cutting.   *Makes 8 servings*

Tip: Lay a paper towel or clean kitchen towel over the vegetables in the colander and weigh them down with a bowl or heavy cans. Let vegetables drain for 1 to 2 hours before preparing recipe. Or roast the sliced vegetables for 10 minutes in a preheated 350°F oven.

herbed chicken and pasta with spanish olives

      4 ounces uncooked gluten-free rotini pasta
      3 tablespoons extra virgin olive oil, divided
    12 ounces boneless skinless chicken breasts, cut into bite-size pieces
      ½ teaspoon dried rosemary
      ¼ teaspoon dried thyme
      ¼ teaspoon red pepper flakes
      4 cloves garlic, minced
      1 cup grape tomatoes, quartered
      3 ounces Spanish stuffed olives, halved lengthwise (about ½ cup)
      2 tablespoons chopped fresh parsley
    1½ cups packed baby spinach, coarsely chopped
      ½ teaspoon salt

1. Cook pasta according to package directions; drain and return to saucepan.

2. Meanwhile, heat 1 tablespoon oil in large skillet over medium-high heat. Cook and stir chicken, rosemary, thyme and red pepper flakes 2 minutes or until chicken is slightly pink in center. Add garlic; cook and stir 15 seconds.

3. Stir in tomatoes, olives and parsley; cook until heated through.

4. Add chicken mixture, spinach, remaining 2 tablespoons oil and salt to pasta; toss until spinach begins to wilt.   *Makes 4 servings*

southern border meat loaf

      1 pound ground beef
      1 can (8 ounces) gluten-free tomato sauce, divided
    ½ cup finely chopped yellow onion
    ½ cup cornmeal
    ¼ cup chopped fresh cilantro
      1 can (4 ounces) chopped mild green chiles
      1 egg, beaten
  1 ½ teaspoons ground cumin
    ½ teaspoon salt
    ¼ teaspoon black pepper
      2 tablespoons ketchup

1. Preheat oven to 350°F. Combine beef, half of tomato sauce, onion, cornmeal, cilantro, chiles, egg, cumin, salt and pepper in mixing bowl; mix well. Combine remaining tomato sauce and ketchup in small bowl.

2. Place meat mixture on greased jelly-roll pan; shape into 6×9-inch oval. Top with tomato sauce mixture.

3. Bake 55 minutes or until cooked through (160°F). Let stand 5 minutes before slicing.   *Makes 4 servings*

sausage and polenta casserole

1 tablespoon olive oil

1 cup chopped mushrooms

1 red bell pepper, diced

1 onion, diced

1 pound bulk Italian sausage

1 jar (28 to 30 ounces) meatless gluten-free pasta sauce

1 roll (16 to 18 ounces) polenta

¼ cup grated Parmesan cheese

1. Preheat oven to 350°F. Spray 8-inch square baking dish with nonstick cooking spray.

2. Heat oil in large skillet. Add mushrooms, bell pepper and onion; cook and stir over medium heat 5 minutes or until tender. Add sausage; cook and stir until sausage is brown, breaking into small pieces with spoon. Drain fat. Stir in pasta sauce; simmer 5 minutes.

3. Cut polenta crosswise into 9 slices; arrange in prepared casserole. Top with sausage mixture.

4. Bake 15 minutes or until heated through. Sprinkle with Parmesan.

Makes 4 servings

southern fried catfish with hush puppies

2 cups yellow cornmeal, divided

½ cup Gluten-Free All-Purpose Flour Blend (page 5)*

2 teaspoons baking powder

2 teaspoons salt, divided

½ teaspoon xanthan gum

1 cup milk

1 small onion, minced

1 egg, lightly beaten

Vegetable oil

3 tablespoons white rice flour

¼ teaspoon ground red pepper

4 catfish fillets (about 1½ pounds)

*Or use any all-purpose gluten-free flour blend that does not contain xanthan gum.

1. Combine 1½ cups cornmeal, flour blend, baking powder, ½ teaspoon salt and xanthan gum in medium bowl. Stir in milk, onion and egg until well blended. Let stand 5 to 10 minutes before frying.

2. Heat 2 inches of oil in large heavy skillet over medium heat until 375°F on deep-fry thermometer. Combine remaining ½ cup cornmeal, rice flour, remaining 1½ teaspoons salt and red pepper in shallow dish. Coat fish with cornmeal mixture.

3. Fry fish in batches 4 to 5 minutes or until golden brown and fish begins to flake when tested with fork. Drain fish on paper towels. Allow temperature of oil to return to 375°F between batches.

4. For hush puppies, drop batter by tablespoonfuls into hot oil. Fry in batches 2 minutes or until golden brown. Drain on paper towels.

Makes 4 servings

quinoa and shrimp salad

1 cup uncooked quinoa

2 cups water

½ teaspoon salt, divided

1 bag (12 ounces) cooked baby shrimp, thawed and well drained

1 cup cherry or grape tomatoes, halved

¼ cup chopped fresh basil

2 tablespoons capers

2 tablespoons finely chopped green onion

3 tablespoons olive oil

1 to 2 tablespoons lemon juice

1 teaspoon grated lemon peel

⅛ teaspoon black pepper

1. Place quinoa in fine-mesh strainer. Rinse well under cold running water. Bring water and ¼ teaspoon salt to a boil in medium saucepan over high heat. Stir in quinoa. Reduce heat to low; cover and simmer 12 to 14 minutes or until water is absorbed and quinoa is tender.

2. Combine quinoa, shrimp, tomatoes, basil, capers and green onion in large bowl. Whisk oil, lemon juice, lemon peel, pepper and remaining ¼ teaspoon salt in small bowl until blended. Pour over salad; toss gently.

Makes 4 to 6 servings

Tip: Soggy shrimp ruin the texture of this salad. To drain shrimp well, blot dry on paper towels.

On the Side

curried lentils with fruit

 2 quarts water
1 ½ cups dried lentils, rinsed and sorted*
 1 Granny Smith apple, peeled and chopped
 ¼ cup golden raisins
 ¼ cup plain yogurt
 1 teaspoon curry powder
 1 teaspoon salt

Packages of dried lentils occasionally contain grit or tiny stones. Sort through and discard any foreign matter.

1. Combine water and lentils in large saucepan; bring to a boil over high heat. Reduce heat to medium-low. Simmer 20 minutes, stirring occasionally.

2. Stir apple and raisins into saucepan; cook 10 minutes or until lentils are tender. Drain.

3. Place lentil mixture in large bowl. Stir in yogurt, curry powder and salt. *Makes 6 servings*

Tip: Apples brown easily once they are cut. Sprinkle with lemon, apple or grapefruit juice if not using immediately.

sweet potato fries

  1 large sweet potato (about 8 ounces)
  2 teaspoons olive oil
  ¼ teaspoon coarse salt
  ¼ teaspoon black pepper
  ¼ teaspoon ground red pepper
     Honey or maple syrup (optional)

1. Preheat oven to 425°F. Spray baking sheet with nonstick cooking spray.

2. Peel sweet potato; cut lengthwise into long spears. Toss with oil, salt, black pepper and ground red pepper on prepared baking sheet. Arrange potato spears in single layer not touching.

3. Bake 20 to 30 minutes or until lightly browned, turning halfway through baking time. Serve with honey, if desired.   *Makes 2 servings*

double apple and dried cherry salad

  1 large Granny Smith apple, diced
  1 large Gala apple, diced
  ⅓ cup dried cherries
  ½ cup (2 ounces) toasted chopped walnuts
  ¼ cup pineapple juice
  1 tablespoon sugar
  ½ teaspoon ground cinnamon
  ½ teaspoon vanilla
  ¼ teaspoon ground nutmeg
  ¼ teaspoon almond extract

Combine apples, cherries and walnuts in large bowl. Whisk pineapple juice, sugar, cinnamon, vanilla, nutmeg and almond extract in small bowl. Pour over salad; mix well. Let stand 10 minutes before serving to allow flavors to blend.   *Makes 8 servings*

tapioca fruit salad

2 cups fresh pineapple chunks

2 cups quartered fresh strawberries

1 cup diced mango

1 cup fresh blueberries

1 cup fresh blackberries

¾ cup sugar, divided

Grated peel and juice of 1 lime

1½ cups coconut milk

1 cup milk

2 eggs, beaten

¼ cup water

3 tablespoons quick-cooking tapioca

½ teaspoon vanilla

⅛ teaspoon salt

1. Combine pineapple, strawberries, mango, blueberries and blackberries in large bowl. Stir in ¼ cup sugar, lime peel and lime juice; mix well. Cover; refrigerate 2 to 3 hours before serving.

2. Combine coconut milk, milk, remaining ½ cup sugar, eggs, water, tapioca, vanilla and salt in medium saucepan. Let stand 5 minutes. Bring to a boil over medium heat, stirring constantly. Remove from heat. Cool 30 minutes. (Pudding will thicken as it cools.) Serve fruit mixture over tapioca.

Makes 8 servings

cheese grits with chiles and bacon

6 strips bacon

1 to 2 serrano or jalapeño peppers,* minced

1 large shallot or small onion, finely chopped

4 cups gluten-free chicken broth

1 cup uncooked grits**

½ teaspoon salt

¼ teaspoon black pepper

1 cup (4 ounces) shredded Cheddar cheese

½ cup half-and-half

2 tablespoons finely chopped green onion

*Chile peppers can sting and irritate the skin, so wear rubber gloves when handling peppers and do not touch your eyes.
**Use coarse, instant, yellow or stone-ground grits.

Slow Cooker Directions

1. Cook bacon in medium skillet over medium heat until crisp. Drain on paper towels. Crumble 2 strips and place in slow cooker. Crumble and refrigerate remaining bacon.

2. Drain all but 1 tablespoon bacon drippings from skillet. Add serrano pepper and shallot; cook and stir 2 minutes or until shallot is lightly browned. Transfer to slow cooker. Stir broth, grits, salt and black pepper into slow cooker. Cover; cook on LOW 4 hours.

3. Stir in cheese and half-and-half. Sprinkle with green onion and reserved bacon. *Makes 4 servings*

vietnamese beef soup (pho)

¾ pound boneless beef top sirloin or top round steak
4 ounces rice noodles
6 cups gluten-free beef broth
3 cups water
2 tablespoons minced fresh ginger
2 tablespoons gluten-free soy sauce
1 cinnamon stick (3 inches long)
½ cup thinly sliced carrots
2 cups fresh bean sprouts
1 red onion, halved and thinly sliced
½ cup chopped fresh cilantro
½ cup chopped fresh basil
2 minced jalapeño peppers* or 1 to 3 teaspoons chili sauce

Jalapeño peppers can sting and irritate the skin, so wear rubber gloves when handling peppers and do not touch your eyes.

1. Freeze beef 45 minutes or until firm. Place rice noodles in large bowl. Cover with hot water; soak 20 minutes or until soft. Drain.

2. Meanwhile, combine broth, water, ginger, soy sauce and cinnamon stick in large saucepan. Bring to a boil over high heat. Reduce heat to low; cover and simmer 20 minutes. Remove and discard cinnamon stick.

3. Slice beef lengthwise in half, then crosswise into very thin strips. Add noodles and carrots to simmering broth; cook 2 to 3 minutes or until carrots are tender. Add beef and bean sprouts; cook 1 minute or until beef is no longer pink.

4. Remove from heat; stir in red onion, cilantro, basil and jalapeño peppers.   *Makes 6 servings*

Tip: Rice noodles are semi-translucent dried noodles that come in many sizes and have many names, including rice stick noodles, rice-flour noodles and pho noodles. Widths range from very thin (called rice vermicelli) to 1 inch wide. All rice noodles must be soaked to soften and all may be used interchangeably.

millet pilaf

1 tablespoon olive oil

½ onion, finely chopped

½ red bell pepper, finely chopped

1 carrot, finely chopped

2 cloves garlic, minced

1 cup uncooked millet

3 cups water

Grated peel and juice of 1 lemon

¾ teaspoon salt

¼ teaspoon black pepper

2 tablespoons chopped fresh parsley (optional)

1. Heat oil in medium saucepan over medium heat. Add onion, bell pepper, carrot and garlic; cook and stir 5 minutes or until softened. Add millet; cook and stir 5 minutes or until lightly toasted.

2. Stir in water, lemon peel, lemon juice, salt and black pepper; bring to a boil. Reduce heat to low; cover and simmer 30 minutes or until water is absorbed and millet is tender. Cover and let stand 5 minutes. Fluff with fork. Sprinkle with parsley, if desired. *Makes 4 servings*

grilled eggplant roll-ups

4 tablespoons hummus

4 thin slices grilled or roasted eggplant

¼ cup crumbled feta cheese

¼ cup chopped green onions

4 tomato slices

1. Spread 1 tablespoon hummus on each eggplant slice. Top with feta, green onion and tomato.

2. Roll up tightly. Serve immediately. *Makes 2 servings*

cranberry-pumpkin spoonbread

    3 cups milk
    1 cup cornmeal
    6 tablespoons (¾ stick) butter
    2 tablespoons packed light brown sugar
 1 ¼ teaspoons pumpkin pie spice
    1 teaspoon baking powder
  ¾ teaspoon salt
    1 can (15 ounces) solid-pack pumpkin
    4 eggs, separated
    1 cup dried cranberries, coarsely chopped

1. Preheat oven to 350°F. Grease 11×7-inch baking pan. Bring milk to a simmer in medium saucepan over medium-high heat. Slowly whisk in cornmeal, stirring until thickened. Remove from heat and stir in butter.

2. Whisk brown sugar, pumpkin pie spice, baking powder and salt in small bowl. Stir into cornmeal mixture until well blended; cool slightly. Stir in pumpkin, egg yolks and cranberries until well blended.

3. Beat egg whites in large bowl with electric mixer at high speed until stiff peaks form. Fold egg whites into cornmeal mixture in three additions. Spoon into prepared pan.

4. Bake 35 minutes or until puffed and golden. Serve warm.

Makes 8 servings

mandarin chicken salad

3½ ounces thin rice noodles (rice vermicelli)
1 can (6 ounces) mandarin orange segments, chilled
⅓ cup honey
2 tablespoons rice wine vinegar
2 tablespoons gluten-free soy sauce
1 can (8 ounces) sliced water chestnuts, drained
4 cups shredded Napa cabbage
1 cup shredded red cabbage
½ cup sliced radishes
4 thin slices red onion, cut in half and separated
3 boneless skinless chicken breasts (about 12 ounces), cooked and cut into strips

1. Place rice noodles in large bowl. Cover with hot water; soak 20 minutes or until soft. Drain.

2. Drain mandarin orange segments, reserving ⅓ cup liquid. Whisk reserved liquid, honey, vinegar and soy sauce in medium bowl. Add water chestnuts.

3. Divide noodles, cabbages, radishes and onion evenly among four serving plates. Top with chicken and orange segments. Remove water chestnuts from dressing and arrange on salads. Serve with remaining dressing.   *Makes 4 servings*

toasted coconut-pecan sweet potato casserole

2 cans (15 ounces each) sweet potatoes in heavy syrup, drained
½ cup (1 stick) butter, softened
¼ cup packed brown sugar
1 egg
½ teaspoon vanilla
⅛ teaspoon salt
½ cup chopped pecans
¼ cup flaked coconut
2 tablespoons golden raisins

1. Preheat oven to 325°F. Spray 8-inch square baking dish with nonstick cooking spray.

2. Combine sweet potatoes, butter, brown sugar, egg, vanilla and salt in food processor or blender; process until smooth. Spoon into prepared dish. Sprinkle evenly with pecans, coconut and raisins.

3. Bake 22 to 25 minutes or until coconut is light golden brown.

Makes 4 servings

Let's Celebrate

marinated citrus shrimp

1 pound (about 32) large cooked shrimp, peeled and deveined, tails on

2 oranges, peeled and separated into segments

1 can (5½ ounces) pineapple chunks in juice, drained and ¼ cup juice reserved

2 green onions, sliced

½ cup orange juice

2 tablespoons minced fresh cilantro

2 tablespoons lime juice

2 tablespoons white wine vinegar

1 tablespoon olive or vegetable oil

1 clove garlic, minced

½ teaspoon dried basil

½ teaspoon dried tarragon

White pepper (optional)

1. Combine shrimp, orange segments, pineapple chunks and green onions in resealable food storage bag. Mix orange juice, reserved pineapple juice, cilantro, lime juice, vinegar, oil, garlic, basil and tarragon in medium bowl; pour over shrimp mixture, turning to coat. Season with white pepper, if desired.

2. Marinate in refrigerator 2 hours or up to 8 hours. Serve as an appetizer or first course. *Makes 16 servings*

tamales

1 package dried corn husks (8 husks)

4 ounces quesadilla cheese or mozzarella cheese

1 can (about 7 ounces) pickled jalapeños

1 can (about 15 ounces) yellow corn, drained, liquid reserved

2 tablespoons butter, softened

1 teaspoon salt

1 cup plus 3 tablespoons cornmeal

Salsa, pico de gallo or guacamole

1. Soak corn husks in warm water 1 hour or until softened.

2. Cut cheese into 4-inch-long strips. Cut jalapeños into strips. Tear narrow strips of corn husk to use as ties for tamales.*

3. Combine corn and 2 tablespoons reserved corn liquid in food processor; pulse until paste forms. Add 1 cup cornmeal, butter and salt; pulse 1 minute or until dough forms. Add more cornmeal gradually until dough is soft and moist, but not sticky. Transfer dough to work surface and keep covered to prevent drying out.

4. Pat corn husk dry. Place 2 tablespoons cornmeal mixture in center of husk. Pat dough into rectangle about 4×2 inches. Arrange 1 strip of cheese and 1 strip of jalapeño in center of dough.

5. Lift sides of husk to enclose filling in dough and wrap gently around tamale. Fold bottom of husk over tamale; tie closed with strip of husk. Tie top closed or leave open. Transfer tamales to steamer basket.

6. Fill large saucepan with water to a depth that will not touch bottom of steamer basket. Bring to a boil. Place steamer basket over water. Cover; steam 45 minutes to 1 hour or until tamale no longer sticks to corn husk, adding additional water to saucepan as needed.

7. Serve tamales with salsa. Tamales may also be refrigerated or frozen and reheated in steamer or microwave.   *Makes 8 tamales*

*You can also secure tamales with kitchen twine, if desired.

green bean casserole with homemade french fried onions

3 cups water

1 pound fresh green beans, cut into 2-inch pieces

1 tablespoon vegetable oil

8 ounces cremini mushrooms, chopped

3 tablespoons butter

3 tablespoons rice flour

1 teaspoon salt

¼ teaspoon red pepper flakes

1 cup gluten-free mushroom or vegetable broth

1 cup whole milk

Homemade French Fried Onions (page 67)

1. Preheat oven to 350°F. Spray 13×9-inch baking dish with nonstick cooking spray.

2. Bring water to a boil in medium saucepan. Add green beans; cook 4 minutes. Drain.

3. Heat oil in large saucepan over medium heat. Add mushrooms; cook and stir 8 minutes. Add butter; cook and stir until melted. Stir in rice flour, salt and red pepper flakes. Slowly stir in broth and milk; cook until thickened. Remove from heat; stir in green beans. Pour into prepared dish.

4. Bake 30 minutes. Meanwhile, prepare Homemade French Fried Onions.

5. Remove casserole from oven. Top with Homemade French Fried Onions; bake 5 minutes. *Makes 6 to 8 servings*

homemade french fried onions

2 small onions, sliced into rings
½ cup milk
½ cup rice flour
½ cup cornmeal
1 teaspoon salt
½ teaspoon black pepper
1 cup vegetable oil

1. Line baking sheet with paper towels. Separate onion rings and spread in shallow baking dish. Pour milk over onions; toss to coat. Combine rice flour, cornmeal, salt and pepper in large food storage bag; mix well.

2. Heat oil in large heavy skillet over medium-high heat until temperature registers 300°F to 325°F on deep-fry thermometer.

3. Working in batches, add onion rings to food storage bag; shake to coat. Using slotted spoon, add onions to oil. Fry 2 minutes per side until golden brown. Remove to baking sheet. Repeat with remaining onions.

wild mushroom quinoa stuffing

1 cup uncooked quinoa

2 tablespoons olive oil, divided

2 cups gluten-free vegetable broth

1 teaspoon poultry seasoning

$\frac{1}{2}$ teaspoon salt

1 small onion, diced

8 ounces cremini mushrooms, sliced

8 ounces shiitake mushrooms, stemmed and sliced

$\frac{1}{2}$ cup diced celery

2 tablespoons chopped fresh parsley (optional)

1. Place quinoa in fine-mesh strainer; rinse well under cold running water.

2. Heat 1 tablespoon oil in medium saucepan over medium-high heat. Add quinoa; stir until evenly coated. Stir in broth, poultry seasoning and salt. Bring to a boil. Reduce heat to low; cover and simmer 15 to 20 minutes or until broth is absorbed and quinoa is tender.

3. Meanwhile, heat remaining 1 tablespoon oil in large skillet over medium heat. Add onion, mushrooms and celery; cook and stir 8 to 10 minutes or until vegetables are tender.

4. Combine quinoa and vegetables in large bowl. Sprinkle with parsley, if desired.   *Makes 6 servings*

lemon-rosemary roasted chicken

1 (6- to 7-pound) chicken

1 tablespoon olive oil

1 teaspoon salt, divided

¼ teaspoon black pepper

2 lemons

2½ teaspoons dried rosemary or 2 (4-inch) sprigs fresh rosemary,
   leaves chopped, divided

1 tablespoon butter, softened

1 large onion, cut into ½-inch slices

¾ cup gluten-free chicken broth

½ teaspoon ground sage

1. Preheat oven to 450°F. Rub chicken with oil. Season with ½ teaspoon salt and pepper.

2. Pierce 1 lemon in several places with knife tip or fork; place in chicken cavity. Blend 2 teaspoons rosemary and butter in small bowl. Carefully slide fingers under skin on breast to loosen. Gently smooth butter mixture under skin. Tie legs with kitchen twine, if desired.

3. Place onion slices in center of roasting pan and place chicken on top. Roast 45 minutes, then tent breast with foil. Roast 30 to 40 minutes longer or until internal temperature reaches 165°F; baste with pan drippings occasionally.

4. Transfer chicken to cutting board; let rest 10 minutes. Pour pan drippings into measuring cup; skim off fat. Squeeze juice from second lemon and add to drippings.

5. Return drippings to roasting pan; add any drippings from chicken. Add remaining ½ teaspoon salt, ½ teaspoon rosemary, broth and sage. Simmer over medium-high heat 2 minutes, scraping up browned bits from bottom of pan. Carve chicken; serve with sauce.   *Makes 8 to 10 servings*

fruit cake

2 cups Gluten-Free All-Purpose Flour Blend (page 5),* plus
   additional for pan

1½ teaspoons xanthan gum

1 teaspoon baking powder

1 teaspoon grated fresh ginger

1 teaspoon ground cinnamon

½ teaspoon baking soda

½ teaspoon salt

½ teaspoon ground cloves

2 cups packed dark brown sugar

1 cup (2 sticks) butter, softened

6 eggs

½ cup orange juice

¼ cup molasses

2 cups golden raisins

1½ cups chopped dried apricots

1 cup chopped walnuts

1 cup chopped pecans

1 cup dried cranberries

Powdered sugar (optional)

*Or use any all-purpose gluten-free flour blend that does not contain xanthan gum.

1. Preheat oven to 300°F. Grease 10-inch bundt pan; dust with flour blend. Combine 2 cups flour blend, xanthan gum, baking powder, ginger, cinnamon, baking soda, salt and cloves in medium bowl.

2. Beat brown sugar and butter in large bowl with electric mixer at medium-high speed 3 minutes or until light and fluffy. Add eggs, one at a time, beating at medium speed until well blended after each addition. Add orange juice and molasses; beat at low speed until well blended. Gradually add flour mixture; beat at medium speed 2 minutes. Fold in raisins, apricots, walnuts, pecans and cranberries. Pour into prepared pan.

3. Bake 2 to 2½ hours or until toothpick inserted near center comes out clean.** Cool in pan on wire rack 1 hour. Remove to wire rack; cool completely. Sprinkle with powdered sugar, if desired.

Makes 12 servings

**If cake becomes too dark on top, tent loosely with foil for last 30 to 60 minutes of baking time.

Note: You can use any combination of your favorite dried fruits and nuts in this recipe.

dark chocolate raspberry bread pudding

8 slices gluten-free bread, cut into ½-inch cubes
¼ cup (½ stick) butter, melted
2 cups whole milk
4 eggs
¾ cup sugar
1 teaspoon vanilla
½ cup raspberries
½ cup bittersweet or semisweet chocolate chips

1. Grease 9-inch baking dish.

2. Combine bread cubes and butter in prepared dish; toss to coat.

3. Whisk milk, eggs, sugar and vanilla in medium bowl. Pour over bread cubes. Cover and refrigerate 2 hours.

4. Preheat oven to 350°F. Sprinkle raspberries and chocolate chips evenly over bread mixture.

5. Bake 40 to 50 minutes or until golden brown and center is set. Let stand 10 minutes before serving.

Makes 6 to 8 servings

vegetarian sushi maki

4 to 6 sheets toasted sushi nori
1 teaspoon wasabi or prepared mustard
1 ½ cups cooked Sushi Rice (recipe follows)
1 ripe avocado, thinly sliced
4 thin strips peeled cucumber
1 cup spinach leaves, thinly sliced
½ cup thinly sliced carrot, steamed
4 teaspoons toasted sesame seeds
Pickled ginger
Gluten-free soy sauce

1. Place 1 sheet of nori on flat work surface. Cover bottom third of sheet with thin layer of wasabi. Spread about ⅓ cup rice on top of wasabi, leaving 1-inch border along bottom edge. Place one quarter each of avocado, cucumber, spinach, carrot and sesame seeds on top of rice.

2. Moisten top edge of nori sheet. Lift bottom edge and press into rice. Roll up and press gently to seal. Repeat with remaining ingredients.

3. Cut rolls crosswise into 1-inch slices with sharp knife, wiping knife with warm water if it gets sticky. Serve with pickled ginger and soy sauce.

Makes 4 to 6 rolls

Sushi Rice: Bring 1¾ cups of water and ½ teaspoon salt to a boil in medium saucepan. Stir in 1 cup uncooked short-grain sushi rice. Reduce heat to low; cover and simmer 20 minutes or until water is absorbed. Remove from heat; let stand 5 minutes. Transfer to shallow bowl. Sprinkle with ⅓ cup seasoned rice vinegar; stir gently.

cheese soufflé

¼ cup (½ stick) butter
¼ cup sweet rice flour (mochiko)
1½ cups milk, warmed to room temperature
¼ teaspoon salt
¼ teaspoon ground red pepper
⅛ teaspoon black pepper
6 eggs, separated
1 cup (4 ounces) shredded Cheddar cheese
Pinch cream of tartar (optional)

1. Preheat oven to 375°F. Grease four 2-cup soufflé dishes or one 2-quart soufflé dish.

2. Melt butter in large saucepan over medium-low heat. Add rice flour; whisk 2 minutes or until mixture just begins to color. Gradually whisk in milk. Add salt, red pepper and black pepper; whisk until mixture comes to a boil and thickens. Remove from heat. Stir in egg yolks, one at a time, and cheese.

3. Beat egg whites and cream of tartar in large bowl with electric mixer at high speed until stiff peaks form.

4. Gently fold egg whites into cheese mixture until almost combined. (Some streaks of white should remain.) Transfer to prepared dishes.

5. Bake small soufflés about 20 minutes (30 to 40 minutes for large soufflé) or until puffed and browned and wooden skewer inserted into center comes out moist but clean. Serve immediately.

Makes 4 servings

cheddar crackers

1 ½ cups brown rice flour
1 teaspoon garlic powder
1 teaspoon salt-free Italian seasoning
½ teaspoon salt
½ cup (2 ounces) finely grated sharp Cheddar cheese
6 tablespoons (¾ stick) cold butter, cut into ½-inch cubes
½ cup water

1. Combine brown rice flour, garlic powder, Italian seasoning and salt in food processor or blender; process until well blended. Add cheese and butter; pulse until evenly incorporated. Add water; process until dough forms.

2. Divide dough in half; wrap in plastic wrap and refrigerate 20 minutes.

3. Preheat oven to 350°F. Line baking sheets with parchment paper.

4. Place each dough half between two pieces of parchment paper; roll out to 1⁄16-inch thickness. Refrigerate 3 to 5 minutes.

5. Cut dough into 2½-inch squares; place on prepared baking sheets.

6. Bake 15 minutes or until golden and crisp, rotating baking sheets after 10 minutes. Cool on baking sheets 10 minutes. Remove to wire racks; cool completely. *Makes 24 crackers*

Safe Sweets

coconut rice pudding

2 cups water
1 cup uncooked converted long grain rice
1 tablespoon butter
Pinch salt
2¼ cups evaporated milk
1 can (14 ounces) cream of coconut
½ cup golden raisins
3 egg yolks, beaten
Grated peel of 2 limes
1 teaspoon vanilla
Toasted shredded coconut (optional)

Slow Cooker Directions

1. Bring water, rice, butter and salt to a boil in medium saucepan over high heat, stirring frequently. Reduce heat to low. Cover; cook 10 to 12 minutes. Remove from heat. Let stand, covered, 5 minutes.

2. Spray slow cooker with nonstick cooking spray. Add evaporated milk, cream of coconut, raisins, egg yolks, lime peel and vanilla; mix well. Add rice; stir until blended.

3. Cover; cook on LOW 4 hours or on HIGH 2 hours, stirring every 30 minutes, if possible. Pudding will thicken as it cools. Garnish with toasted shredded coconut, if desired.   *Makes 6 servings*

thumbprint cookies

1 cup (2 sticks) butter, softened

½ cup packed dark brown sugar

2 egg yolks

2 teaspoons vanilla

2 cups Gluten-Free All-Purpose Flour Blend (page 5)*

½ teaspoon salt

2 egg whites, beaten

2¼ cups chopped walnuts

¼ cup raspberry jam

*Or use any all-purpose gluten-free flour blend that does not contain xanthan gum.

1. Preheat oven to 375°F. Line cookie sheets with parchment paper.

2. Beat butter and brown sugar in large bowl with electric mixer at medium-high speed 2 minutes or until light and fluffy. Add egg yolks and vanilla; beat at low speed, scraping side of bowl as needed. Beat in flour blend and salt just until combined.

3. Place egg whites in shallow dish. Place walnuts in separate shallow dish. Roll tablespoonfuls of dough into balls; dip in egg whites and roll in walnuts. Place on prepared cookie sheets.

4. Using back of small spoon or thumb, make small indentation in center of each ball; fill with jam.

5. Bake 12 to 15 minutes or until golden brown and filling is set, rotating cookie sheets halfway through baking time. Cool on cookie sheets 5 minutes. Remove to wire racks; cool completely.

Makes 2 dozen cookies

cranberry pear cobbler

Filling

    3 pounds ripe pears (6 pears), peeled and sliced
1½ cups cranberries
  ¼ cup granulated sugar
    1 tablespoon cornstarch
    1 tablespoon grated orange peel
    1 teaspoon ground cinnamon

Topping

    1 package (about 15 ounces) gluten-free yellow cake mix
    1 cup buttermilk
  ½ cup (1 stick) butter, softened
    2 teaspoons vanilla
1½ tablespoons granulated sugar
1½ tablespoons packed brown sugar
    Whipped cream (optional)

1. Preheat oven to 400°F. Spray 13×9-inch baking dish with nonstick cooking spray.

2. Combine pears, cranberries, ¼ cup granulated sugar, cornstarch, orange peel and cinnamon in large bowl; toss to coat. Pour into prepared baking dish.

3. Bake about 20 minutes or until bubbly.

4. Meanwhile, beat cake mix, buttermilk, butter and vanilla in large bowl with electric mixer at low speed 30 seconds or until moistened. Beat at medium speed 2 minutes. Pour evenly over filling. Sprinkle with 1½ tablespoons granulated sugar and brown sugar.

5. Bake 30 to 35 minutes or until topping is golden brown. Serve warm with whipped cream, if desired. *Makes 8 servings*

caramel chocolate tart

Crust

>¾ cup Gluten-Free All-Purpose Flour Blend (page 5)*, plus additional
>for work surface
>
>¾ cup unsweetened cocoa powder
>
>½ cup (1 stick) cold butter, cubed
>
>3 tablespoons sugar
>
>½ teaspoon xanthan gum
>
>⅛ teaspoon salt
>
>3 tablespoons whipping cream
>
>1 egg
>
>1 egg yolk

Filling

>1 cup sugar
>
>¼ cup water
>
>2 tablespoons light corn syrup
>
>5 tablespoons butter
>
>¼ cup whipping cream
>
>1 teaspoon vanilla

Ganache

>½ cup plus 1 tablespoon whipping cream
>
>4 ounces bittersweet chocolate, chopped

Or use any all-purpose gluten-free flour blend that does not contain xanthan gum.

1. For crust, beat ¾ cup flour blend, cocoa, ½ cup butter, 3 tablespoons sugar, xanthan gum and salt in large bowl with electric mixer at medium speed until mixture resembles coarse crumbs. Beat in 3 tablespoons cream, egg and egg yolk just until combined. Wrap in plastic wrap; refrigerate at least 1 hour or up to 3 days.

2. Roll dough into 10-inch circle (about ¼ inch thick) on floured surface. Press into 9-inch tart pan. Trim edges to fit pan. Prick bottom with fork. Cover and refrigerate 30 minutes.

3. Preheat oven to 350°F. Line tart shell with foil and fill with pie weights or dried beans. Bake 15 minutes.

4. Remove foil and weights. Bake 10 to 12 minutes. Remove to wire rack; cool completely.

5. For filling, combine 1 cup sugar, water and corn syrup in large saucepan; cook and stir over medium-high heat until sugar is completely melted and deep amber color. Remove from heat.

6. Whisk in 5 tablespoons butter, ¼ cup cream and vanilla. Let stand 5 minutes to cool slightly. Pour into cooled crust. Let stand 45 minutes or until set.

7. For ganache, bring ½ cup plus 1 tablespoon cream to a simmer in small saucepan. Place chocolate in large bowl. Whisk cream into chocolate until smooth and well blended.

8. Pour ganache over filling, tilting to cover completely. Refrigerate 2 hours or until set. *Makes 8 servings*

no-bake cherry crisps

    1 cup powdered sugar
    1 cup peanut butter
    ¼ cup (½ stick) butter, softened
 1⅓ cups gluten-free crisp rice cereal
    ½ cup maraschino cherries, drained, dried and chopped
    ¼ cup plus 2 tablespoons mini semisweet chocolate chips
    ¼ cup chopped pecans
    2 cups flaked coconut

1. Beat powdered sugar, peanut butter and butter in large bowl with electric mixer at medium speed until blended. Stir in cereal, cherries, chocolate chips and pecans.

2. Shape teaspoonfuls of mixture into 1-inch balls. Roll in coconut. Place on cookie sheets and refrigerate 1 hour. Store cookies between sheets of waxed paper in airtight container in refrigerator.

Makes about 3 dozen cookies

polenta apricot pudding cake

¼ cup chopped dried apricots

1½ cups orange juice

1 cup ricotta cheese

3 tablespoons honey

¾ cup sugar

⅔ cup cornmeal

½ cup Gluten-Free All-Purpose Flour Blend (page 5)*

¾ teaspoon xanthan gum

½ teaspoon salt

¼ teaspoon ground nutmeg

½ cup slivered almonds

*Or use any all-purpose gluten-free flour blend that does not contain xanthan gum.

1. Preheat oven to 325°F. Spray 9-inch nonstick springform pan with nonstick cooking spray.

2. Soak apricots in warm water in small bowl 15 minutes to soften. Drain and pat dry. Set aside.

3. Beat orange juice, ricotta cheese and honey in large bowl with electric mixer at medium speed 5 minutes or until smooth. Combine sugar, cornmeal, flour blend, xanthan gum, salt and nutmeg in medium bowl. Add to orange juice mixture; mix well. Stir in apricots. Pour into prepared pan. Sprinkle with almonds.

4. Bake 40 to 50 minutes or until center is almost set and cake is golden brown. Serve warm. *Makes 8 servings*

lemon cheesecake

Crust

   5 tablespoons butter, softened

   ¼ cup sugar

   1½ teaspoons grated lemon peel

   1 cup Gluten-Free All-Purpose Flour Blend (page 5)*

   1 teaspoon xanthan gum

   ⅛ teaspoon salt

Filling

   1 envelope (2¾ teaspoons) unflavored gelatin

   ¼ cup water

   12 ounces cream cheese, softened

   ¾ cup sugar

   ⅓ cup lemon juice

   1 cup whipping cream, at room temperature

Topping

   ¼ cup sugar

   2 egg yolks

   1 egg

   3 tablespoons lemon juice

   ⅛ teaspoon salt

   3 tablespoons butter

   Grated lemon peel (optional)

Or use any all-purpose gluten-free flour blend that does not contain xanthan gum.

1. Preheat oven to 350°F. Line bottom of 9-inch springform pan with foil or parchment paper; spray with nonstick cooking spray.

2. For crust, beat 5 tablespoons butter, ¼ cup sugar and 1½ teaspoons lemon peel in large bowl with electric mixer at medium speed 2 minutes or until light and fluffy. Beat in flour blend, xanthan gum and ⅛ teaspoon salt at low speed until mixture resembles coarse crumbs. Press mixture onto bottom of prepared pan. Bake 10 to 12 minutes or until golden brown. Cool completely in pan on wire rack.

3. Meanwhile for filling, sprinkle gelatin over water in small microwavable bowl. Let stand 5 minutes or until gelatin softens. Microwave on HIGH 30 seconds or until gelatin is dissolved and mixture bubbles around edge.

4. Beat cream cheese and ¾ cup sugar in large bowl with electric mixer at medium-high speed until well blended. Beat in ⅓ cup lemon juice at low speed until well blended. Add cream; beat at medium-high speed 2 minutes or until fluffy. Add gelatin; beat 3 minutes or until well combined. Pour mixture over crust. Cover and refrigerate until set.

5. For topping, combine ¼ cup sugar, egg yolks, egg, 3 tablespoons lemon juice and ⅛ teaspoon salt in small saucepan; cook and stir over medium-low heat 3 minutes or until thickened. Remove from heat.

6. Stir in 3 tablespoons butter until well blended and butter is melted. Pour mixture through fine-mesh strainer into medium bowl. Let stand 5 minutes to cool slightly.

7. Spread cooled lemon topping over cheesecake. Cover and refrigerate 4 hours or until set. Garnish with lemon peel.

Makes 10 to 12 servings

lemony arrowroot cookies

Cookies

- ¼ cup (½ stick) butter
- ⅓ cup granulated sugar
- 1 egg
  Grated peel and juice of 1 lemon
- ½ teaspoon vanilla
- 1¼ cups Gluten-Free All-Purpose Flour Blend (page 5),* plus additional for work surface
- ½ cup arrowroot
- ½ teaspoon baking powder
- ¼ teaspoon salt

Glaze

- ¼ cup powdered sugar
- 1 teaspoon grated lemon peel, plus additional for garnish
- 1 tablespoon lemon juice, plus additional if necessary

*Or use any all-purpose gluten-free flour blend that does not contain xanthan gum.

1. Preheat oven to 350°F. Grease cookie sheet or line with parchment paper.

2. Beat butter and granulated sugar in large bowl with electric mixer at medium speed until creamy. Add egg, grated peel and juice of 1 lemon and vanilla; beat until well blended. Add 1¼ cups flour blend, arrowroot, baking powder and salt; beat at low speed just until combined.

3. Roll out dough on floured surface to ⅛-inch thickness. Cut out shapes with cookie cutters. Place 2 inches apart on prepared cookie sheet.

4. Bake 8 to 10 minutes. (Cookies will not brown.) Remove to wire rack; cool completely.

5. Combine powdered sugar and 1 teaspoon lemon peel in small bowl; stir in enough lemon juice to make pourable glaze. Drizzle glaze over cookies. Garnish with additional lemon peel.   *Makes 12 cookies*

white chocolate pudding with crunchy toffee topping

¼ cup sugar

1¾ teaspoons guar gum*

¼ teaspoon salt

2 cups reduced-fat (2%) milk

¾ cup whipping cream

7 squares (1 ounce each) white chocolate, chopped

2 teaspoons vanilla

Crunchy Toffee Topping (recipe follows)

Or substitute ¼ cup cornstarch for guar gum.

1. Combine sugar, guar gum and salt in medium saucepan; mix well. Slowly whisk in milk and cream. Bring to a boil over medium heat, stirring constantly. Reduce heat; cook and stir 2 to 3 minutes or until mixture is thickened.

2. Remove from heat; stir in white chocolate and vanilla until chocolate is completely melted. Spoon into six dessert dishes; cover with plastic wrap. Refrigerate 1 hour or up to 2 days.

3. Prepare Crunchy Toffee Topping. Sprinkle over pudding just before serving. *Makes 6 servings*

crunchy toffee topping

½ cup sugar

¼ cup light corn syrup

1 cup sliced almonds

2 teaspoons butter

½ teaspoon baking soda

½ teaspoon vanilla

1. Spray 10-inch square sheet of foil with nonstick cooking spray.

2. Whisk sugar and corn syrup in small microwavable bowl. Microwave on HIGH 4 minutes. (Mixture will be light brown in color.) Stir in almonds and butter; microwave on HIGH 2 minutes. Stir in baking soda and vanilla. (Mixture will foam.)

3. Spread mixture in thin layer on prepared foil; cool completely. Break into pieces.

crispy cupcakes

¼ cup (½ stick) plus 2 tablespoons butter, divided

1 package (10½ ounces) marshmallows

½ cup creamy peanut butter

6 cups gluten-free crisp rice cereal

1 cup bittersweet or semisweet chocolate chips

1½ cups powdered sugar

¼ cup milk

1. Spray 13×9-inch baking pan with nonstick cooking spray. Microwave 2 tablespoons butter in large microwavable bowl on HIGH 30 seconds or until melted. Add marshmallows; stir until coated with butter. Microwave on HIGH 1 minute; stir. Microwave 45 seconds; stir until melted. Stir in peanut butter until well blended. Add cereal; stir until blended.

2. Spread mixture in prepared pan, using waxed paper to spread and press into even layer. Let stand 10 to 15 minutes or until set.

3. Meanwhile, place remaining ¼ cup butter and chocolate chips in medium microwavable bowl. Microwave on HIGH 40 seconds; stir. Microwave at additional 15-second intervals until melted and smooth. Gradually beat in powdered sugar and milk until well blended. Refrigerate until ready to use.

4. Spray 1½-inch round cookie or biscuit cutter with nonstick cooking spray; cut out 36 circles from cereal bars. Place small dab of frosting on top of 18 circles; top with remaining 18 circles, pressing down firmly to seal. Place "cupcakes" in paper baking cups, if desired. Pipe or spread frosting on cupcakes. *Makes 18 cupcakes*

Contents

cooking dairy-free and easy

Two Kinds of Sensitivity

1. Lactose Intolerance

Lactose is the natural sugar in milk. Many people don't produce enough of an enzyme (lactase) to properly digest lactose. When they drink milk, they experience symptoms like stomach pain or diarrhea. If you are lactose-intolerant, you may be able to enjoy some dairy. Cheese and butter tend to be

lower in lactose than milk. This is because they contain less milk sugar (but more fat). You are the best judge of what works for you.

2. Milk Allergy

As with other true allergies, being allergic to milk means that your immune system overreacts to a protein—usually casein or whey in this case. Symptoms of a milk allergy can be mild or as severe and life-threatening as anaphylactic shock. If you have a true milk allergy, it's important to avoid all dairy in any form.

Be a Label Detective

Did you know that most margarine contains dairy? Are you aware that hydrolyzed casein and whey powder are dairy products? Fortunately, U.S. food manufacturers are now required to list the simple word "milk" as

part of the ingredient list or in boldface type at the end of the list, even if the actual ingredient goes by an obscure chemical name. The recent popularity of the vegan diet is a boon for the dairy-free shopper, too. Since vegans consume no animal products, you can assume products labeled vegan are dairy-free. The kosher designation "pareve" is another handy indicator that the product contains no milk.

Celebrate the Naturally Dairy-Free

It's more fun to find new things you CAN eat than to concentrate on the forbidden. Asian cuisines tend to be mostly dairy-free. Japanese sushi, teriyaki and noodle dishes are perfect examples. Chinese menus offer plenty of ideas, too. Most stir-fries, noodle dishes and sauces contain no dairy. And many of them are also gluten-free! Using coconut milk as they do in Thai dishes is a wonderful way to enjoy the rich creaminess missing from some dairy-free cooking.

You Won't Miss the Moo

Going dairy-free might be one of the healthiest things you can do for your diet. You'll be eating less animal fat and probably fewer calories. With a bit of planning and the recipes in this book, dairy-free meals can be easy, nutritious and delicious.

Non-Dairy is NOT always Dairy-Free

Many products labeled non-dairy contain whey, casein or other milk-derived ingredients. According to the FDA, non-dairy products can contain 0.5% or less of milk products by weight. Non-dairy creamers and non-dairy whipped toppings usually contain dairy in some form.

the dairy-free pantry

Cooking dairy-free is easier if you keep these staples on hand:

- ❏ avocado
- ❏ cheese alternatives (read labels carefully)
- ❏ chocolate and chips, dairy-free semisweet
- ❏ cocoa powder, unsweetened
- ❏ coconut butter or oil
- ❏ coconut milk, unsweetened
- ❏ creamer, dairy-free
- ❏ hummus
- ❏ margarine, dairy-free (read labels carefully)
- ❏ nutritional yeast
- ❏ olive oil (extra virgin)
- ❏ soymilk, rice milk, almond milk
- ❏ tahini
- ❏ tofu, silken and regular
- ❏ vegetable shortening

Dairy-Free Dairy Stand-Ins

1. Bread crumbs sautéed in extra virgin olive oil until crisp are a great topper for pasta or casseroles instead of cheese.

2. Go Italian. Instead of butter, add fresh herbs and a sprinkle of freshly ground black pepper to a shallow dish of extra virgin olive oil for dipping crusty bread.

3. Mashed avocado or hummus (try plain or flavored varieties) make a sandwich spread with more flavor and better nutrition than butter.

4. Make your favorite dips with silken tofu instead of sour cream. They'll be just as creamy without the animal fat.

5. Need buttermilk? Add 1 tablespoon of lemon juice to 1 cup of soymilk. Let it stand for a few minutes to curdle and you can use it, one-to-one, to replace buttermilk in pancakes or baked goods.

6. Try Whipped Coconut Cream Topping to replace whipped cream or non-dairy whipped topping (despite the name, many brands contain casein).

whipped coconut cream topping

1 can (14 ounces) high quality unsweetened coconut milk (not "light")

2 to 3 tablespoons powdered sugar

1 tablespoon tapioca flour

1 teaspoon vanilla

1. Refrigerate can of coconut milk, standing upright, for at least 10 hours. Place medium bowl and beaters from mixer in freezer overnight.

2. Open can of coconut milk carefully without shaking. Spoon coconut cream from top into cold bowl. Beat with electric mixer using cold beaters at high speed until thickened. Add powdered sugar to taste, tapioca flour and vanilla. Beat about 2 minutes or until soft peaks form. Refrigerate until needed.   *Makes about ⅔ cup*

But What about Cheese?!

Giving up cheese is one of the toughest challenges for many who go dairy-free. In addition to providing flavor, cheese melts, stretches and binds ingredients together in unique ways. Mimicking these qualities isn't easy. Fortunately, there are more and better dairy-free cheeses available every year. It's now possible to find dairy-free cheese in blocks, sliced, shredded or grated. Always check ingredients lists carefully. There are some lactose-free cheeses that are considered nondairy, but they invariably contain casein. Try a variety of brands to find those that suit your needs and your taste buds.

You can also create your own substitutes for some cheeses using tofu or nutritional yeast. Here are three recipes to get you started.

dairy-free cheez sauce

¾ cup nutritional yeast
¼ cup all-purpose flour
1½ teaspoons salt
¼ teaspoon garlic powder
¼ teaspoon onion powder

2 cups unsweetened soymilk or other dairy-free milk
1 teaspoon prepared yellow mustard
3 drops hot sauce (optional)

1. Combine nutritional yeast, flour, salt, garlic powder and onion powder in medium saucepan. Whisk in soymilk over medium heat until smooth.

2. Add mustard and hot sauce, if desired. Whisk 10 minutes or until mixture thickens to desired consistency. Mix with cooked pasta or serve over green vegetables, baked potatoes or corn chips.

Makes about 1¾ cups

Tip: Mix with any cooked pasta and vegetables for a quick dish. Try Cheez Sauce over vegetables or corn chips, too.

not-ricotta

1 package (14 ounces) firm tofu, pressed
1 cup silken tofu
½ cup chopped parsley

2 teaspoons kosher salt
2 teaspoons lemon juice
1 teaspoon sugar
1 teaspoon black pepper

Crumble firm tofu into large bowl. Add silken tofu, parsley, salt, lemon juice, sugar and pepper; mix well. Refrigerate until needed. Drain liquid before using.

Makes 3 cups

dairy-free feta

1 package (14 ounces) firm or extra firm tofu
¼ cup extra virgin olive oil
2 tablespoons lemon juice
2 teaspoons Greek or Italian seasoning

1½ teaspoons salt
1 teaspoon onion powder
½ teaspoon garlic powder
½ teaspoon black pepper

1. Cut tofu crosswise into 2 pieces, each about 1 inch thick. Place on cutting board lined with paper towels; top with layer of paper towels. Place weighted baking dish on top of tofu. Let stand 20 minutes. Pat tofu dry and crumble into large bowl.

2. Combine oil, lemon juice, Greek seasoning, salt, onion powder, garlic powder and black pepper in small jar with lid; shake to combine well. Pour over tofu and toss gently. Refrigerate 2 hours or overnight.

Makes about 2 cups

Good Mornings

egg & sausage casserole

8 ounces bulk pork sausage

3 tablespoons dairy-free margarine, divided

2 tablespoons all-purpose flour

¼ teaspoon salt

¼ teaspoon black pepper

1¼ cups dairy-free milk

2 cups frozen hash brown potatoes, thawed

4 eggs, hard-cooked and sliced

½ cup cornflake crumbs

¼ cup sliced green onions

1. Preheat oven to 350°F. Spray 2-quart baking dish with nonstick cooking spray.

2. Brown sausage in large skillet over medium-high heat 6 to 8 minutes, stirring to break up meat. Drain fat. Transfer to plate.

3. Melt 2 tablespoons margarine in same skillet over medium heat. Stir in flour, salt and pepper until smooth. Gradually stir in dairy-free milk; cook and stir until thickened. Add sausage, potatoes and eggs; stir until blended. Transfer to prepared baking dish.

4. Melt remaining 1 tablespoon margarine in small saucepan over low heat. Add cornflake crumbs; stir until combined. Sprinkle evenly over casserole.

5. Bake 30 minutes or until hot and bubbly. Sprinkle with green onions just before serving. *Makes 6 servings*

vegan pancakes

2 cups soymilk or other dairy-free milk

2 tablespoons lemon juice

2 tablespoons vegetable oil

1 tablespoon agave nectar

1 cup all-purpose flour

1 cup spelt flour

1 teaspoon baking soda

1 teaspoon baking powder

½ teaspoon salt

1 to 2 tablespoons dairy-free margarine, melted

Fresh fruit or maple syrup

1. Combine soymilk and lemon juice in large measuring cup or medium bowl. Set aside 5 minutes or until curdled. Stir in oil and agave.

2. Whisk all-purpose flour, spelt flour, baking soda, baking powder and salt in large bowl. Whisk in soymilk mixture until fairly smooth. (Some lumps will remain.)

3. Heat large nonstick skillet or griddle over medium high heat. Brush lightly with margarine. Pour batter into skillet in 4-inch circles. Cook 3 to 5 minutes until edges of pancake become dull and bubbles form on top. Turn over; cook 1 to 2 minutes or until browned. Keep warm.

4. Serve with fresh fruit or maple syrup.   *Makes about 14 pancakes*

california omelet with avocado

2 plum tomatoes, chopped

2 to 4 tablespoons chopped fresh cilantro

¼ teaspoon salt

8 eggs

¼ cup dairy-free milk

1 ripe avocado, diced

1 cucumber, chopped

1. Preheat oven to 200°F. Combine tomatoes, cilantro and salt in small bowl; set aside.

2. Whisk eggs and dairy-free milk in medium bowl until well blended.

3. Heat small nonstick skillet over medium heat; spray with nonstick cooking spray. Pour half of egg mixture into skillet; cook 2 minutes or until eggs begin to set. Lift edge of omelet to allow uncooked portion to flow underneath. Cook 3 minutes or until set.

4. Spoon half of tomato mixture over half of omelet. Loosen omelet with spatula and fold in half. Slide omelet onto serving plate and keep warm in oven. Repeat for second omelet. Top with avocado and cucumber.

Makes 2 to 4 servings

french toast with marmalade

⅓ cup dairy-free margarine, softened

2 tablespoons orange marmalade

2 teaspoons honey

4 eggs, beaten

½ cup dairy-free milk

2 tablespoons sugar

1 teaspoon ground cinnamon

1 teaspoon vanilla

¼ teaspoon ground nutmeg

8 ounces French bread, cut diagonally into 8 slices

2 tablespoons vegetable oil

Powdered sugar

1. Combine margarine, marmalade and honey in small bowl until well blended; set aside.

2. Whisk eggs, dairy-free milk, sugar, cinnamon, vanilla and nutmeg in shallow bowl. Heat 1 tablespoon oil in large skillet over medium heat. Dip bread slices into egg mixture.

3. Cook bread in single layer 3 minutes per side or until golden, adding additional oil as needed.

4. Sprinkle with powdered sugar. Serve with marmalade mixture.

Makes 4 servings

potato and pork frittata

12 ounces (about 3 cups) frozen hash brown potatoes

1 teaspoon Cajun seasoning

4 egg whites

2 eggs

¼ cup dairy-free milk

1 teaspoon dry mustard

¼ teaspoon black pepper

10 ounces (about 3 cups) frozen stir-fry vegetable blend

⅓ cup water

¾ cup chopped cooked lean pork

½ cup (2 ounces) shredded dairy-free Cheddar cheese alternative

1. Preheat oven to 400°F. Spray baking sheet with nonstick cooking spray. Spread potatoes on prepared baking sheet; sprinkle with Cajun seasoning. Bake 15 minutes or until hot. Remove from oven. *Reduce oven temperature to 350°F.*

2. Beat egg whites, eggs, dairy-free milk, mustard and pepper in small bowl. Place vegetables and water in medium ovenproof nonstick skillet; cook over medium heat 5 minutes or until vegetables are crisp-tender; drain.

3. Stir potatoes and pork into vegetables. Add egg mixture; sprinkle with dairy-free cheese. Cook over medium-low heat 5 minutes. Place skillet in oven; bake 5 minutes or until eggs are set. Cut into 4 wedges.

Makes 4 servings

sunny seed bran waffles

2 egg whites
1 tablespoon dark brown sugar
1 tablespoon canola or vegetable oil
1 cup dairy-free milk
⅔ cup wheat bran
⅔ cup quick oats
1½ teaspoons baking powder
¼ teaspoon salt
3 tablespoons sunflower seeds, toasted*
1 cup apple butter

To toast sunflower seeds, cook and stir in small nonstick skillet over medium heat about 5 minutes or until golden brown. Remove from skillet; let cool.

1. Beat egg whites in medium bowl with electric mixer at high speed until soft peaks form. Blend brown sugar and oil in small bowl. Stir in dairy-free milk; mix well.

2. Combine bran, oats, baking powder and salt in large bowl; mix well. Stir milk mixture into bran mixture. Add sunflower seeds; stir just until moistened. *Do not overmix.* Gently fold in beaten egg whites.

3. Spray nonstick waffle iron lightly with nonstick cooking spray; heat according to manufacturer's directions. Stir batter; spoon ½ cup batter into waffle iron for each waffle. Cook until steam stops escaping from around edges and waffle is golden brown. Serve each waffle with ¼ cup apple butter.   *Makes 4 waffles*

Note: It is essential to use a nonstick waffle iron because of the low fat content of these waffles.

chocolate cherry pancakes

    2 cups all-purpose flour
    1 cup dried cherries
    ⅔ cup dairy-free semisweet chocolate chips
    ⅓ cup sugar
  4½ teaspoons baking powder
    ½ teaspoon baking soda
    ½ teaspoon salt
  1½ cups dairy-free milk
    2 eggs
    ¼ cup (½ stick) dairy-free margarine, melted

1. Combine flour, dried cherries, chocolate chips, sugar, baking powder, baking soda and salt in large bowl; mix well. Beat dairy-free milk, eggs and margarine in medium bowl until well blended.

2. Add milk mixture to flour mixture; stir just until moistened. (Add ¼ to ½ cup additional dairy-free milk for thinner pancakes.)

3. Heat griddle or large nonstick skillet over medium heat until drop of water sizzles when dropped on surface. Pour ¼ cupfuls of batter onto griddle. Cook 2 to 3 minutes. Turn over; cook 2 to 3 minutes or until or until golden. *Makes 6 to 8 servings*

eggs benedict with smoked salmon

Dairy-Free Hollandaise Sauce (recipe follows)

4 dairy-free English muffins, split and toasted

4 ounces sliced smoked salmon

8 tomato slices

1 teaspoon white vinegar

8 eggs

Chopped fresh dill

1. Preheat oven to 200°F. Prepare Dairy-Free Hollandaise and keep warm. Place 2 muffin halves, split side up, on each of 4 serving plates. Divide smoked salmon among muffin halves. Top with tomato slices. Place plates in oven; turn off oven.

2. Fill large skillet with 2 inches of water; add vinegar and bring to a simmer over medium heat. Break 4 eggs into 4 ramekins or small bowls. Holding ramekins close to surface, slip eggs into water.

3. Cook eggs 3 minutes or until whites are completely set and yolks begin to thicken. Remove eggs with slotted spoon; drain well. Place eggs on prepared muffin halves. Repeat with remaining eggs. Spoon Dairy-Free Hollandaise Sauce over each egg. Sprinkle with fresh dill; serve immediately. *Makes 4 servings*

dairy-free hollandaise sauce

½ cup (1 stick) dairy-free margarine

3 egg yolks

1 tablespoon lemon juice

½ teaspoon dry mustard

2 to 3 drops hot sauce (optional)

Melt margarine in small saucepan over low heat. Combine egg yolks, lemon juice, mustard and hot sauce, if desired, in blender or food processor. With motor running, add margarine in thin stream through feed tube. *Makes about ⅔ cup*

peanut butter and jelly french toast

1 banana, sliced

2 tablespoons peanuts, chopped

2 tablespoons orange juice

1 tablespoon honey

6 slices dairy-free whole wheat bread

¼ cup grape jelly (or favorite flavor)

¼ cup peanut butter

2 eggs

¼ cup dairy-free milk

2 tablespoons dairy-free margarine

1. Combine banana, peanuts, orange juice and honey in small bowl; set aside. Spread three slices of bread with jelly and three slices with peanut butter. Press peanut butter and jelly slices together to form three sandwiches; cut each sandwich in half diagonally.

2. Melt margarine on large nonstick griddle or skillet over medium-high heat. Beat eggs and dairy-free milk in shallow bowl. Dip sandwiches in egg mixture. Cook 2 minutes on each side or until lightly browned.

3. Top with banana mixture just before serving.   *Makes 3 servings*

mediterranean artichoke omelet

2 eggs

1 tablespoon vegan Parmesan-flavor topping

2 tablespoons olive oil

3 canned water-packed artichoke bottoms, drained, diced

¼ cup diced roasted red bell pepper

½ teaspoon minced garlic

Salsa

1. Beat eggs in small bowl. Stir in Parmesan-flavor topping.

2. Heat oil in large nonstick skillet over medium-high heat. Add artichokes; cook and stir 2 to 3 minutes or until beginning to brown. Add pepper; cook and stir 2 minutes or until liquid has evaporated. Add garlic; cook and stir 30 seconds. Remove to small plate; keep warm.

3. Add egg mixture to skillet. Lift edge of omelet with spatula to allow uncooked portion to flow underneath. Cook 1 to 2 minutes or until omelet is almost set.

4. Spoon artichoke mixture onto half of omelet; fold omelet over filling. Cook 2 minutes or until set. Serve with salsa.   *Makes 1 serving*

Note: Raw eggs will turn green if combined with raw artichokes because of a chemical reaction between the two foods. Cooking the artichokes separately and then folding them into the eggs will prevent that.

Small Plates

thai beef salad

    8 ounces flank steak
    ¼ cup soy sauce
    2 jalapeño peppers,* finely chopped
    2 tablespoons packed brown sugar
    1 clove garlic, minced
    ½ cup lime juice
    6 green onions, thinly sliced
    4 carrots, diagonally cut into thin slices
    ½ cup finely chopped fresh cilantro
       Lettuce leaves

Jalapeño peppers can sting and irritate the skin, so wear rubber gloves when handling peppers and do not touch your eyes.

1. Place flank steak in resealable food storage bag. Combine soy sauce, jalapeños, brown sugar and garlic in small bowl; pour over flank steak. Seal bag; turn to coat. Marinate in refrigerator 2 hours.

2. Preheat broiler. Drain steak; discard marinade. Place steak on rack of broiler pan. Broil 4 inches from heat 13 to 18 minutes for medium or to desired doneness, turning once. Remove from heat; let stand 15 minutes.

3. Thinly slice steak across grain. Toss with lime juice, green onions, carrots and cilantro in large bowl. Serve salad immediately over lettuce leaves.   *Makes 4 servings*

herbed chicken dijon sliders

    1 pound ground chicken
    ⅓ cup chopped green onions
    2 tablespoons Worcestershire sauce
1 ½ to 2 teaspoons chopped fresh thyme
    1 clove garlic, minced
    ¼ cup Dijon mustard
  12 dairy-free whole wheat dinner rolls, cut in half
    2 cups mixed salad greens
    1 tomato, cut into 12 thin slices

1. Mix chicken, green onions, Worcestershire sauce, thyme and garlic in large bowl. Shape into 12 (½-inch-thick) patties.

2. Spray large skillet with nonstick cooking spray; heat over medium heat. Cook patties 4 to 5 minutes on each side or until cooked through (165°F).

3. Spread bottom halves of buns with 1 teaspoon Dijon mustard and top with salad greens. Place burgers on greens; top with tomato slices and top halves of buns.   *Makes 12 sliders*

mediterranean pita pizzas

¼ cup Dairy-Free Feta (recipe follows)
1 cup chopped, peeled cucumber
1 to 2 tablespoons lemon juice
1 tablespoon chopped fresh oregano
4 (6-inch) dairy-free pita bread rounds, warmed
½ cup roasted red pepper hummus
½ cup chopped tomato
¼ cup sliced olives

1. Prepare Dairy-Free Feta.

2. Combine cucumber, lemon juice and oregano in small bowl.

3. Spread hummus evenly over pita. Top with cucumber mixture, tomato, olives and Dairy-Free Feta. *Makes 4 servings*

dairy-free feta

1 package (about 14 ounces) firm or extra firm tofu
¼ cup extra virgin olive oil
2 tablespoons lemon juice
2 teaspoons salt
1½ teaspoons Greek or Italian seasoning
1 teaspoon onion powder
½ teaspoon black pepper
½ teaspoon garlic powder

1. Cut tofu crosswise into 2 pieces, each about 1 inch thick. Place on cutting board lined with paper towels; top with layer of paper towels. Place weighted baking dish on top of tofu. Let stand 30 minutes to drain. Pat tofu dry and crumble into large bowl.

2. Combine oil, lemon juice, salt, Greek seasoning, salt, onion powder, garlic powder and black pepper in small jar with lid; shake until well blended. Pour over tofu and toss gently. Refrigerate 2 hours or overnight.
Makes about 2 cups

herbed turkey meatballs

½ cup coarsely chopped green bell pepper

⅓ cup chopped parsley

3 tablespoons dill pickle relish

2 egg whites

1 teaspoon dried basil

1 teaspoon dried oregano

½ teaspoon salt

½ teaspoon black pepper

1 pound ground turkey

¼ cup oats

1 tablespoon olive oil

Hot Tomato Dipping Sauce (recipe follows)

1. Place bell pepper, parsley, relish, egg whites, basil, oregano, salt and black pepper in food processor. Pulse until bell pepper is finely minced. Add turkey and oats; pulse 2 or 3 times or just until mixed. Chill mixture 15 minutes.

2. Preheat oven to 325°F. Shape tablespoonfuls of turkey mixture into egg-shaped meatballs. Heat oil in nonstick skillet over medium heat. Brown meatballs on all sides. Place on nonstick baking sheet.

3. Bake 10 to 15 minutes or until cooked through. Meanwhile, prepare Hot Tomato Dipping Sauce; serve with meatballs. *Makes 16 meatballs*

hot tomato dipping sauce

½ cup vegetable broth

½ cup chopped tomato

2 tablespoons tomato paste

1 teaspoon Italian seasoning

Hot pepper sauce (optional)

Combine broth, tomato, tomato paste and Italian seasoning in small saucepan. Bring to a simmer over low heat. Season with hot pepper sauce, if desired.

tarragon potato salad

6 medium unpeeled red potatoes (about 1¾ pounds), scrubbed

1 cup frozen peas, thawed

¾ cup chopped green bell pepper

¾ cup mayonnaise

¼ cup dairy-free milk

¼ cup sliced green onions

2 tablespoons chopped fresh parsley

1 tablespoon lemon juice

2 teaspoons dried tarragon

½ teaspoon salt

¼ teaspoon black pepper

1. Place potatoes in large saucepan; add water to cover. Bring to a boil. Reduce heat to low; cover and simmer 25 minutes or until tender. Drain and set aside until cool enough to handle.

2. Slice potatoes and place in large bowl. Stir in peas and bell pepper. Combine mayonnaise, dairy-free milk, green onions, parsley, lemon juice, tarragon, salt and black pepper in small bowl. Pour over vegetables; stir gently to coat. Cover and refrigerate at least 4 hours.

Makes 6 to 8 servings

Tip: Mayonnaise looks creamy but is almost always free of dairy. It does contain eggs, so if that is a concern, look for a mayo that is labeled "vegan." It will be egg-free.

parsnip patties

1 pound parsnips, peeled and cut into ¾-inch chunks

4 tablespoons (½ stick) dairy-free margarine, divided

¼ cup chopped onion

¼ cup all-purpose flour

⅓ cup dairy-free milk

2 teaspoons chopped fresh chives

Salt and black pepper

¾ cup fresh bread crumbs

2 tablespoons vegetable oil

1. Pour 1 inch water into medium saucepan; bring to a boil over high heat. Add parsnips; cover and cook 10 minutes or until fork-tender. Drain. Place in large bowl; coarsely mash with fork.

2. Melt 2 tablespoons margarine in small skillet over medium-high heat. Add onion; cook and stir until translucent. Whisk in flour until bubbly and lightly browned. Whisk in dairy-free milk until thickened; stir into mashed parsnips. Stir in chives; season with salt and pepper.

3. Shape parsnip mixture into four patties. Spread bread crumbs on plate. Dip patties in bread crumbs to coat all sides evenly. Place on waxed paper and refrigerate 2 hours.

4. Heat remaining 2 tablespoons margarine and oil in large skillet over medium-high heat until butter is margarine and bubbly. Add patties; cook 5 minutes on each side or until browned.   *Makes 4 servings*

california ham rolls

2 cups water

½ teaspoon salt, divided

1 cup short grain brown rice

2 tablespoons unseasoned rice vinegar* or cider vinegar

1 tablespoon sugar

4 (8-inch) sheets sushi nori wrappers*

8 thin strips ham (about 4 ounces)

¼ cup reduced-sodium soy sauce

1 tablespoon mirin (sweet rice wine)*

1 tablespoon minced chives

These ingredients can be found in the Asian section of the supermarket.

1. Bring water and ¼ teaspoon salt to a boil in medium saucepan over high heat. Stir in rice. Reduce heat to low; cover and simmer 40 to 45 minutes or until water is absorbed and rice is tender but chewy. Spoon rice into large shallow bowl.

2. Combine vinegar, sugar and remaining ¼ teaspoon salt in small bowl. Microwave on HIGH 30 seconds. Stir to dissolve sugar. Pour over rice; stir to mix well. Set aside to cool.

3. Place 1 sheet of nori on work surface. Loosely spread about ½ cup rice over nori, leaving ½-inch border. Place 2 strips of ham along width of nori. Moisten top edge of nori sheet. Roll up tightly. Gently press to redistribute rice, if necessary. Cut into 6 slices with sharp knife. Place cut side up on serving plate. Repeat with remaining nori, rice and ham.

4. Combine soy sauce and mirin in small bowl. Sprinkle with chives. Serve with ham rolls.   *Makes 4 servings*

crispy ranch chicken bites

Dairy-Free Ranch Dressing (recipe follows), **divided**
1 pound boneless skinless chicken breasts
2 cups panko bread crumbs

1. Prepare Dairy-Free Ranch Dressing.

2. Preheat oven to 375°F. Line baking sheet with foil; spray foil with olive oil cooking spray.

3. Cut chicken into 1-inch cubes. Place ¾ cup ranch dressing in small bowl. Spread panko in shallow dish. Dip chicken in ranch dressing; shake off excess. Transfer to panko; press to coat all sides. Place breaded chicken on prepared baking sheets. Spray with cooking spray.

4. Bake 15 to 17 minutes or until golden brown and cooked through, turning once. Serve with remaining ranch dressing.   *Makes 4 servings*

dairy-free ranch dressing

4 teaspoons soymilk or other dairy-free milk
¾ teaspoon lemon juice
1 cup egg-free (vegan) mayonnaise
1 tablespoon chopped fresh parsley
1 tablespoon chopped fresh chives
½ teaspoon dried dill weed
¼ teaspoon onion powder
¼ teaspoon salt
⅛ teaspoon ground black pepper

1. Combine soymilk and lemon juice in small bowl. Let stand 10 minutes.

2. Meanwhile, whisk mayonnaise, parsley, chives, dill weed, onion powder, salt and pepper in medium bowl. Stir in soymilk mixture; refrigerate at least 30 minutes to blend flavors.   *Makes about 1¼ cups*

grilled halibut sandwiches with creamy cilantro ranch dressing

¼ cup Dairy-Free Ranch Dressing (page 136)

1 tablespoon chopped fresh cilantro

1 teaspoon grated lime peel

2 tablespoons lime juice

4 halibut fillets

2 teaspoons Southwest seasoning

4 dairy-free rolls or bread

Tomato slices and arugula

1. Prepare Dairy-Free Ranch Dressing. Blend ranch dressing, cilantro and lime peel in small bowl; set aside.

2. Spray indoor grill or grill pan with nonstick cooking spray. Heat grill. Drizzle lime juice over fish; sprinkle with Southwest seasoning. Grill 3 to 4 minutes or until fish begins to flake when tested with fork.

3. Serve fish on rolls; top with ranch dressing, tomatoes and arugula.

Makes 4 servings

Pasta & Pizza Please!

grilled vegetable pizzas

2 tablespoons olive oil

1 clove garlic, minced

1 red bell pepper, cut into quarters

4 slices red onion, cut ¼ inch thick

1 medium zucchini, halved lengthwise

1 medium yellow squash, halved lengthwise

1 cup dairy-free pizza sauce

¼ teaspoon red pepper flakes

2 (10-inch) prepared pizza crusts

2 cups (8 ounces) shredded dairy-free mozzarella cheese alternative

¼ cup sliced fresh basil leaves

1. Prepare grill for direct cooking.

2. Combine oil and garlic in small bowl; brush over bell pepper, onion, zucchini and squash. Grill vegetables, covered, over medium heat 10 minutes or until crisp-tender, turning halfway through grilling time.

3. Cut bell pepper lengthwise into ¼-inch strips. Cut zucchini and squash crosswise into ¼-inch slices. Separate onion slices into rings.

4. Combine pizza sauce and red pepper flakes in small bowl; spread over crusts. Top with dairy-free mozzarella and grilled vegetables.

5. Grill pizzas, covered, over medium-low heat 5 to 6 minutes or until hot. Sprinkle with basil; cut into wedges. *Makes 8 servings*

tofu stuffed shells

1 can (15 ounces) tomato purée

8 ounces mushrooms, thinly sliced

½ cup shredded carrot

¼ cup water

2 cloves garlic, minced

1 tablespoon sugar

1 tablespoon Italian seasoning

12 uncooked jumbo pasta shells

1 package (14 ounces) firm tofu, drained and pressed

½ cup chopped green onions

2 tablespoons vegan Parmesan-flavor topping

2 tablespoons minced parsley

1 tablespoon dried basil

½ teaspoon salt

¼ teaspoon black pepper

½ cup (2 ounces) shredded dairy-free mozzarella cheese alternative

1. For sauce, combine tomato purée, mushrooms, carrot, water, garlic, sugar and Italian seasoning in medium saucepan. Bring to a boil over medium heat. Reduce heat to low; cover and simmer 20 minutes, stirring occasionally.

2. Meanwhile, cook shells according to package directions. Rinse under cold water; drain. Preheat oven to 350°F. Spread thin layer of sauce in bottom of 11×8-inch baking pan.

3. Crumble tofu into medium bowl. Stir in green onions, Parmesan-flavor topping, parsley, basil, salt and pepper. Stuff shells with tofu mixture. Place shells, stuffed side up, in single layer in prepared pan. Pour remaining sauce evenly over shells.

4. Cover tightly with foil; bake 30 minutes. Remove foil; sprinkle with dairy-free mozzarella. Bake, uncovered, 5 to 10 minutes or until hot and bubbly.

Makes 4 servings

grilled pizza margherita with beer-risen crust

¾ cup beer

1 package (¼ ounce) active dry yeast

2 tablespoons plus 2 teaspoons extra virgin olive oil, divided

1¾ to 2½ cups all-purpose flour

1 teaspoon salt

1½ pints grape tomatoes, halved

1 clove garlic, minced

¼ teaspoon dried basil

⅛ teaspoon salt

⅛ teaspoon red pepper flakes

6 ounces dairy-free mozzarella cheese alternative (solid pack), cut into slices

10 fresh basil leaves, thinly sliced

1. Microwave beer in small microwavable bowl on HIGH 25 seconds. Stir in yeast and 2 teaspoons oil; let stand 5 minutes or until foamy. Combine 1¾ cups flour and salt in medium bowl. Add beer mixture to flour mixture and stir until dough pulls away from sides of bowl, adding additional flour as needed. Turn out dough onto floured surface; knead 6 to 7 minutes or until smooth and elastic. Divide dough in half and shape into balls. Dust with flour; place in separate medium bowls. Cover; let rise in warm, draft-free place about 1½ hours or until doubled in bulk.

2. Heat 1 tablespoon oil in medium nonstick skillet over medium-high heat. Add tomatoes, garlic, basil, salt and red pepper flakes; cook 3 to 4 minutes or until tomatoes are very soft, stirring occasionally. Set aside.

3. Preheat grill for direct cooking over high heat. Oil grid.

4. Working with one ball at a time, turn dough onto lightly floured surface. Gently stretch dough into 9-inch round. Transfer to floured baking sheets. Brush tops of each round with half of remaining oil. Cover; let stand 10 minutes.

5. *Reduce grill to medium heat.* Carefully flip dough rounds onto grid, oiled side down. Grill, uncovered, 3 minutes or until bottoms are golden and well marked. Turn crusts; spread with tomato mixture, leaving ½-inch border. Top with dairy-free mozzarella; cover and grill 3 minutes or until cheese begins to melt and crust is golden brown. Transfer to cutting board; sprinkle with basil. *Makes 4 servings*

spicy manicotti

3 cups Not-Ricotta (page 101)

⅔ cup vegan Parmesan-flavor topping, plus additional for serving

1 egg, lightly beaten

2½ tablespoons chopped fresh parsley

1 teaspoon Italian seasoning

½ teaspoon garlic powder

½ teaspoon salt

½ teaspoon black pepper

1 pound spicy Italian sausage

1 can (28 ounces) crushed tomatoes, undrained

1 jar (26 ounces) marinara sauce

8 ounces uncooked manicotti pasta

1. Preheat oven to 375°F. Spray 13×9-inch baking dish with nonstick cooking spray.

2. For filling, combine Not-Ricotta, ⅔ cup Parmesan-flavor topping, egg, parsley, Italian seasoning, garlic powder, salt and pepper in medium bowl; set aside.

3. Crumble sausage into large skillet; brown over medium-high heat until no longer pink, stirring to separate meat. Drain sausage on paper towels; drain fat from skillet.

4. Add tomatoes with juice and marinara sauce to same skillet; bring to a boil over high heat. Reduce heat to low; simmer, uncovered, 10 minutes. Pour about one third of sauce into prepared dish.

5. Stuff each shell with about ½ cup filling. Place in dish. Top shells with sausage; pour remaining sauce over shells.

6. Cover tightly with foil; bake 50 minutes to 1 hour or until pasta is tender. Let stand 5 minutes before serving. Sprinkle with additional Parmesan-flavor topping.   *Makes 8 to 10 servings*

neapolitan pizza

½ to ¾ cup warm water (105° to 115°F)

1 package (¼ ounce) active dry yeast

1 teaspoon sugar

2 cups all-purpose flour

1 tablespoon olive oil

½ teaspoon salt

1 cup dairy-free pizza sauce

2 cups (8 ounces) shredded dairy-free mozzarella cheese alternative

4 ounces sliced pepperoni (about 1 cup)

1 small green bell pepper, seeded and sliced

1 small onion, thinly sliced

¼ cup vegan Parmesan-flavor topping

1. Combine ¼ cup water, yeast and sugar in small bowl. Stir to dissolve yeast; let stand about 5 minutes or until bubbly.

2. Measure flour, oil and salt into food processor. Process 5 seconds. Add yeast mixture; process 10 seconds or until blended.

3. Turn on processor and very slowly drizzle just enough remaining water through feed tube so dough forms a ball that cleans side of bowl. Process until ball turns around bowl about 25 times. Let dough stand 1 to 2 minutes.

4. Turn on processor and gradually drizzle in enough remaining water to make dough soft, smooth and satiny but not sticky. Process until dough turns around bowl about 15 times.

5. Turn dough onto greased 14-inch pizza pan or large baking sheet. Shape dough into ball. Cover with inverted bowl or plastic wrap and let stand 10 minutes.

6. Preheat oven to 425°F. Roll out or pat dough to cover pan, making slight rim around edge. Spread sauce evenly over dough. Top with sauce, dairy-free mozzarella, pepperoni, bell pepper, onion and Parmesan-flavor topping. Bake 15 to 20 minutes or until crust is golden.

Makes 4 servings

kale, mushroom and caramelized onion pizza

1 package (13.8 ounces) refrigerated pizza dough

1 tablespoon olive oil

1 cup chopped yellow onion

1 package (8 ounces) sliced mushrooms

3 cloves garlic, minced

4 cups packed coarsely chopped kale

¼ teaspoon red pepper flakes

½ cup dairy-free pizza sauce

¾ cup (3 ounces) shredded dairy-free mozzarella cheese alternative

1. Preheat oven to 425°F. Spray 15×10-inch jelly-roll pan with nonstick cooking spray. Unroll pizza dough on prepared pan. Press dough evenly into pan and ½ inch up sides. Prick dough all over with fork. Bake 7 to 10 minutes or until lightly browned.

2. Heat oil in large nonstick skillet over medium heat. Add onion; cook and stir 8 minutes or until golden brown. Add mushrooms and garlic; cook and stir 4 minutes. Add kale and red pepper flakes; cover and cook 2 minutes to wilt kale. Uncover; cook and stir 3 to 4 minutes or until vegetables are tender.

3. Spread pizza sauce over crust. Spread kale mixture evenly over sauce; top with dairy-free mozzarella. Bake 10 minutes or until crust is golden brown.   *Makes 4 servings*

vegan artichoke lasagna

1 tablespoon olive oil

1 cup chopped onion

3 cloves garlic, chopped

¼ cup tomato paste

¼ cup white wine

1 can (28 ounces) Italian plum tomatoes, undrained, or crushed tomatoes

1 teaspoon sugar

1 teaspoon kosher salt

1 teaspoon dried oregano

9 uncooked lasagna noodles

Not-Ricotta (page 101)

1 can (14 ounces) artichoke hearts, drained and chopped

1 package (10 ounces) frozen chopped spinach, thawed and squeezed dry

2 cups (8 ounces) shredded dairy-free mozzarella cheese alternative

2 roasted bell peppers, chopped

1. For sauce, heat oil in large saucepan over medium-high heat. Add onion and garlic; cook and stir 5 minutes or until onion is tender. Stir in tomato paste; cook 1 minute. Stir in wine; cook 30 seconds. Add tomatoes with juice, sugar, salt and oregano; break up tomatoes with spoon. Reduce heat; cover and simmer 30 minutes.

2. Cook lasagna noodles according to package directions. Drain and return to saucepan; cover with cold water to prevent sticking.

3. Prepare Not-Ricotta. Combine artichokes and spinach in small bowl.

4. Preheat oven to 350°F. Spray 13×9-inch baking dish with nonstick cooking spray. Spread ½ cup sauce in dish; arrange 3 noodles over sauce. Spread half of Not-Ricotta over noodles; top with artichoke mixture, half of shredded dairy-free mozzarella and ½ cup sauce. Repeat layers of noodles and Not-Ricotta; top with roasted peppers, remaining 3 noodles, sauce and dairy-free mozzarella.

5. Cover with greased foil; bake 45 minutes. Remove foil; bake 15 minutes. Let stand 10 minutes before serving. *Makes 8 servings*

sausage pizza pie casserole

8 ounces mild Italian sausage, casings removed

1 package (13.8 ounces) refrigerated pizza dough

½ cup tomato sauce

2 tablespoons chopped fresh basil or 2 teaspoons dried basil

½ teaspoon dried oregano

¼ teaspoon red pepper flakes

3 ounces mushrooms, quartered

½ cup thinly sliced red onion

½ cup thinly sliced green bell pepper

½ cup seeded diced tomato

½ cup sliced pitted black olives

1½ cups (6 ounces) shredded dairy-free mozzarella
cheese alternative

2 tablespoons vegan Parmesan-flavor topping

1. Preheat oven to 350°F. Spray 13×9-inch baking dish with nonstick cooking spray.

2. Brown sausage in large nonstick skillet over medium-high heat 6 to 8 minutes, stirring to break up meat. Drain fat.

3. Unroll pizza dough in prepared baking dish; press evenly onto bottom and up sides. Spoon sauce evenly over dough; sprinkle with basil, oregano and red pepper flakes. Layer with sausage, mushrooms, onion, bell pepper, tomato, olives and dairy-free mozzarella. Roll down sides of crust to form rim.

4. Bake 20 to 25 minutes or until crust is golden brown. Sprinkle with Parmesan-flavor topping; let stand 5 minutes before serving.

Makes 4 servings

family-style beef pizza

1 package (13.8 ounces) refrigerated pizza dough

¼ pound ground beef

3 tablespoons finely chopped onion

¾ cup dairy-free pizza sauce

1 small tomato, peeled, seeded and chopped

2 teaspoons Italian seasoning

2 cloves garlic, minced

⅛ teaspoon ground red pepper

½ cup sliced mushrooms

1 cup (4 ounces) shredded dairy-free mozzarella cheese alternative

1 tablespoon vegan Parmesan-flavor topping

1. Preheat oven to 425°F. Lightly spray 12-inch pizza pan with nonstick cooking spray. Unroll pizza dough; press onto prepared pan, making slight rim around edge. Prick dough all over with fork. Bake 7 to 10 minutes or until lightly browned.

2. Meanwhile, brown ground beef with onion in large skillet over medium-high heat 6 to 8 minutes, stirring to break up meat. Drain fat.

3. Combine pizza sauce, tomato, Italian seasoning, garlic and red pepper in small saucepan over medium heat; bring to a boil. Reduce heat; simmer 3 minutes.

4. Spread sauce evenly over pizza crust. Sprinkle with ground beef mixture and mushrooms. Sprinkle with dairy-free mozzarella and Parmesan-flavor topping. Bake 5 to 8 minutes or until heated through.

Makes 4 servings

Moo-less Main Dishes

maple salmon and sweets

½ cup pure maple syrup

2 tablespoons dairy-free margarine, melted

1 ½ pounds skin-on salmon fillets

2 medium sweet potatoes, peeled and cut into ¼-inch-thick slices

1 teaspoon salt

¼ teaspoon black pepper

1. Combine maple syrup and margarine in small bowl. Place salmon in resealable food storage bag. Place sweet potatoes in another resealable food storage bag. Pour half of syrup mixture into each bag; seal. Refrigerate at least 2 hours or overnight, turning bags occasionally.

2. Prepare grill for direct cooking. Oil grid. Drain salmon and sweet potatoes; discard marinade. Season with salt and pepper.

3. Grill salmon, skin side down, on covered grill over medium heat 15 to 20 minutes or until fish begins to flake when tested with fork. Grill sweet potatoes, covered, in single layer on grill topper 15 minutes or until tender and slightly browned, turning once or twice.

Makes 4 servings

grilled skirt steak fajitas

1 ½ pounds skirt steak

½ cup pale ale

3 tablespoons lime juice

1 teaspoon ground cumin

2 tablespoons olive oil

1 cup thinly sliced red onion

1 cup thinly sliced red and green bell peppers

2 cloves garlic, minced

3 plum tomatoes, each cut into 4 wedges

1 tablespoon reduced-sodium soy sauce

¾ teaspoon salt

¼ teaspoon black pepper

8 (7-inch) flour tortillas

Avocado slices and salsa (optional)

1. Place steak in large resealable food storage bag. Combine ale, lime juice and cumin in small bowl; pour over steak. Seal bag; turn to coat. Refrigerate 2 hours, turning occasionally.

2. Heat oil in large nonstick skillet over medium-high heat. Add onion; cook and stir 2 to 3 minutes or until beginning to soften. Add bell peppers; cook and stir 7 to 8 minutes or until softened. Add garlic; cook and stir 1 minute. Add tomatoes; cook 2 minutes or just until beginning to soften. Add soy sauce; cook 1 minute. Keep warm.

3. Prepare grill for direct cooking. Lightly oil grid.

4. Remove steak from marinade; discard marinade. Sprinkle with salt and black pepper. Grill over medium-high heat 4 to 6 minutes on each side to 145°F or desired doneness. Transfer to cutting board; cut across grain into ¼-inch-thick slices.

5. Warm tortillas and fill with steak and vegetable mixture. Top with avocado slices and salsa, if desired. *Makes 4 servings*

provençal lemon and olive chicken

2 cups chopped onions

8 skinless chicken thighs (about 2½ pounds)

1 lemon, thinly sliced and seeded

1 cup pitted green olives

1 tablespoon olive brine or white vinegar

2 teaspoons herbes de Provence

1 bay leaf

½ teaspoon salt

⅛ teaspoon black pepper

1 cup chicken broth

½ cup minced fresh Italian parsley

Slow Cooker Directions

1. Place onions in slow cooker. Arrange chicken thighs and lemon slices over onion. Add olives, brine, herbes de Provence, bay leaf, salt and pepper. Pour in broth.

2. Cover; cook on LOW 5 to 6 hours or on HIGH 3 to 3½ hours or until chicken is tender. Stir in parsley before serving.   *Makes 8 servings*

peppered pork cutlets with onion gravy

½ teaspoon paprika

¼ teaspoon ground cumin

¼ teaspoon black pepper

⅛ teaspoon ground red pepper (optional)

4 boneless pork cutlets

1 tablespoon olive oil

2 cups thinly sliced onions

2 tablespoons all-purpose flour, divided

¾ cup water

1½ teaspoons chicken bouillon granules

2 tablespoons dairy-free milk

¼ teaspoon salt

1. Combine paprika, cumin, black pepper and ground red pepper, if desired, in small bowl; mix well. Sprinkle mixture evenly over one side of each cutlet and press down gently. Let stand 15 minutes.

2. Heat oil in large skillet over medium heat. Cook pork, seasoned side down, 3 minutes or until browned. Remove from skillet.

3. Add onions to same skillet. Cook and stir over medium-high heat 3 to 5 minutes or until browned. Stir in 1½ tablespoons flour. Stir in water and bouillon; bring to a boil.

4. Return pork and any accumulated juices to skillet; reduce heat to low. Spoon sauce over pork; cover and simmer 15 to 20 minutes or until pork is barely pink in center.

5. Remove pork to plate; keep warm. Stir dairy-free milk and salt into onion mixture in skillet; cook 1 to 2 minutes. Serve pork with onion gravy.

Makes 4 servings

not your momma's meat loaf

  2 pounds ground beef, pork and veal meat loaf mix
  ⅔ cup plain dry bread crumbs
  ½ cup finely chopped onion
  ½ cup pale ale
  ⅓ cup plus 3 tablespoons ketchup, divided
  2 eggs
  1 tablespoon Dijon mustard
  2 teaspoons dried basil
  1 teaspoon garlic powder
  1 teaspoon salt
  ½ teaspoon black pepper

1. Preheat oven to 350°F. Spray jelly-roll pan with nonstick cooking spray.

2. Combine meat loaf mix, bread crumbs, onion, ale, 3 tablespoons ketchup, eggs, mustard, basil, garlic powder, salt and pepper in large bowl; mix well. Transfer mixture to prepared pan; shape into 10×5×2-inch loaf. Spread remaining ⅓ cup ketchup over top.

3. Bake 60 to 65 minutes or until cooked through (160°F). Let stand 10 minutes before slicing. *Makes 6 servings*

mac and cheez

1 ½ cups uncooked elbow macaroni

1 cup chopped onion

1 cup chopped red or green bell pepper

¾ cup chopped celery

¾ cup nutritional yeast

¼ cup all-purpose flour

1 ½ teaspoons salt

¼ teaspoon garlic powder

¼ teaspoon onion powder

2 cups unsweetened soymilk or other dairy-free milk

1 teaspoon prepared yellow mustard

3 drops hot sauce (optional)

½ teaspoon paprika

1. Preheat oven to 350°F. Spray 12✕8-inch baking dish with nonstick cooking spray. Cook macaroni according to package directions; add onion, bell pepper and celery to water during last 5 minutes of cooking. Drain; return to saucepan.

2. Meanwhile, combine nutritional yeast, flour, salt, garlic powder and onion powder in medium saucepan. Whisk in soymilk over medium heat until smooth. Add mustard and hot sauce, if desired. Whisk 10 minutes or until mixture thickens to desired consistency. Pour over macaroni and vegetables; mix well.

3. Spread mixture in prepared baking dish; sprinkle with paprika. Bake 15 to 20 minutes or until heated through.   *Makes 4 to 6 servings*

salmon cakes with red pepper relish

¾ cup roasted red bell peppers, drained and finely chopped

2 tablespoons chopped Italian parsley

2 teaspoons grated lemon peel, divided

1 tablespoon lemon juice

3 teaspoons olive oil, divided

1 clove garlic, minced

3 cans (6 ounces each) skinless boneless salmon, drained and crumbled

¼ cup plain dry bread crumbs

¼ cup finely chopped green onions

1 egg white

¼ teaspoon black pepper

1. For relish, combine roasted peppers, parsley, 1 teaspoon lemon peel, lemon juice, 1 teaspoon olive oil and garlic in small bowl; set aside.

2. Combine salmon, bread crumbs, green onions, egg white, black pepper and remaining 1 teaspoon lemon peel in medium bowl. Shape ⅓ cupfuls into 8 (2½-inch) cakes.

3. Heat remaining 2 teaspoons oil in large nonstick skillet over medium-high heat. Cook salmon cakes 3 to 4 minutes on each side or until browned. Serve with relish.   *Makes 4 servings*

cantonese tomato beef

1 beef flank steak (about 1 pound)

2 tablespoons soy sauce

2 tablespoons dark sesame oil, divided

1 tablespoon plus 1 teaspoon cornstarch, divided

1 pound Chinese-style thin wheat noodles

1 cup beef broth

2 tablespoons packed brown sugar

1 tablespoon cider vinegar

2 tablespoons vegetable oil, divided

1 tablespoon minced fresh ginger

3 small onions, cut into wedges

2 pounds ripe tomatoes (5 large), cored and cut into wedges

1 green onion, diagonally cut into thin slices

1. Cut flank steak lengthwise in half, then crosswise into ¼-inch-thick slices. Combine soy sauce, 1 tablespoon sesame oil and 1 teaspoon cornstarch in large bowl. Add beef slices; toss to coat. Set aside.

2. Cook noodles according to package directions. Drain; toss with remaining 1 tablespoon sesame oil. Keep warm. Combine broth, brown sugar, remaining 1 tablespoon cornstarch and vinegar in small bowl; set aside.

3. Heat wok over high heat 1 minute. Drizzle 1 tablespoon vegetable oil into wok and heat 30 seconds. Add beef and marinade; stir-fry 5 minutes or until lightly browned. Remove beef from wok; reduce heat to medium. Add ginger and stir-fry 30 seconds.

4. Add remaining 1 tablespoon vegetable oil to wok. Add onion wedges; stir-fry 2 minutes. Stir in half of tomato wedges. Stir broth mixture; add to wok. Cook and stir until liquid boils and thickens.

5. Return beef and any juices to wok. Add remaining tomato wedges; cook and stir until heated through. Serve over noodles.

Makes 4 servings

pork scaloppine

⅓ cup all-purpose flour

¾ teaspoon salt

½ teaspoon black pepper

1 pound pork tenderloin, cut into ½-inch-thick slices

3 tablespoons olive oil, divided

16 ounces sliced mushrooms

½ cup sliced green onions

½ cup water

¼ cup white wine

½ teaspoon dried marjoram

½ teaspoon dried basil

½ cup chopped pimiento-stuffed green olives (optional)

Hot cooked orzo pasta or rice

1. Combine flour, salt and pepper in shallow bowl. Pound pork slices to ¼-inch thickness with meat mallet. Coat each slice with flour mixture; shake off excess.

2. Heat 1 tablespoon oil in large skillet over medium-high heat. Add mushrooms; cook and stir 6 to 8 minutes or until tender. Remove from skillet and keep warm.

3. Heat remaining 2 tablespoons oil in same skillet. Add pork; cook 1 to 2 minutes on each side or until browned. Add green onions, water, wine, marjoram and basil; bring to a simmer. Stir in olives if desired; cover and cook 3 to 4 minutes on each side or until pork is barely pink in center. Remove pork to serving platter.

4. Return mushrooms with any accumulated juices to skillet; cook 2 to 3 minutes or until heated through. Serve pork with sauce and orzo.

Makes 4 to 6 servings

Dairy-Free Desserts

margarita cheesecake

     1 package (16 ounces) silken tofu, drained
     2 packages (8 ounces each) dairy-free cream cheese alternative
     ¾ cup sugar
     2 eggs
     2 tablespoons tequila
     2 tablespoons orange liqueur
        Grated peel and juice of 1 lime
     1 (9-inch) graham cracker crust
     20 to 25 small pretzel sticks, crushed (optional)

1. Preheat oven to 325°F.

2. Place tofu in food processor; process until smooth. Add dairy-free cream cheese and sugar; process until smooth. Add eggs, tequila, liqueur, lime peel and lime juice; process until smooth. Pour into crust.

3. Bake 45 minutes or until edge is firm but center is still soft. Turn off oven; leave door slightly ajar for 1 hour. Cool completely and refrigerate before serving. Sprinkle crushed pretzels around edge of cheesecake, if desired.   *Makes 8 servings*

lemon berry bundt

1 package (about 18 ounces) dairy-free lemon cake mix

5 eggs

1 cup plain soy yogurt

⅓ cup vegetable oil

1 tablespoon grated lemon peel

8 ounces frozen unsweetened mixed berries *or* 1½ cups fresh berries

1 cup powdered sugar

1½ to 2 tablespoons lemon juice

Fresh berries and mint leaves (optional)

1. Preheat oven to 325°F. Spray 10-inch nonstick bundt pan with nonstick cooking spray.

2. Beat cake mix, eggs, soy yogurt, oil and lemon peel in large bowl with electric mixer at low speed 30 seconds or until moistened. Beat at medium speed 2 minutes. Spoon half of batter into prepared pan; sprinkle with berries. Pour remaining batter over berries.

3. Bake 53 to 55 minutes or until toothpick inserted near center comes out clean. Cool in pan on wire rack 15 minutes. Gently loosen edge and center of cake with knife; invert onto wire rack.

4. For glaze, blend powdered sugar and lemon juice in small bowl until smooth. Spoon evenly over cake. Garnish with fresh berries and mint leaves. *Makes 12 to 14 servings*

coconut milk ice cream

2 cans (about 13 ounces each) unsweetened coconut milk
½ cup sugar
1 dairy-free candy bar, crushed into small pieces

1. Combine coconut milk and sugar in medium saucepan. Cook over medium-low heat, whisking constantly, until smooth and sugar is dissolved. Refrigerate until cold.

2. Process in ice cream maker according to manufacturer's directions, adding candy pieces during last 2 minutes. Transfer to freezer container and freeze until firm.

3. To serve, let ice cream soften at room temperature, or microwave 20 to 30 seconds on HIGH. *Makes about 1 quart*

dairy-free pudding ice cream

1 package (8 serving size) instant pudding and pie filling mix*
3 cups dairy-free milk
  Optional additions: nuts, dairy-free chocolate chips or crushed candies

Choose any dairy-free flavor, but check ingredient lists. Not all are dairy-free.

1. Whisk pudding mix and dairy-free milk in large bowl until smooth. Immediately transfer to ice cream maker; process according to manufacturer's directions.

2. Serve immediately or transfer to freezer container. If frozen solid, let ice cream stand at room temperature to soften before serving.

Makes about 6 servings

orange olive oil cake

1 ¾ cups (9 ounces) dairy-free yellow or white cake mix (about half of one 18-ounce package)

¼ cup extra virgin olive oil

1 egg

1 egg white

Grated peel and juice of 2 oranges (about ¾ cup juice), divided

2 tablespoons sugar

2 tablespoons orange liqueur (optional)

Candied orange peel and basil leaves (optional)

1. Preheat oven to 350°F. Spray 8-inch round cake pan with nonstick cooking spray.

2. Beat cake mix, olive oil, egg and egg white in large bowl with electric mixer at low speed 30 seconds or until moistened. Beat at medium speed 2 minutes. Stir in grated orange peel. Pour into prepared pan.

3. Bake about 20 minutes or until cake is golden and toothpick inserted into center comes out clean. Cool in pan on wire rack 5 minutes. Invert cake onto serving platter.

4. Combine orange juice, sugar and liqueur, if desired, in small saucepan; bring to a boil. Reduce heat to medium; cook 10 minutes or until mixture thickens and is reduced to about ¼ cup. Cool slightly.

5. Pour syrup over cake; cool completely before serving. Garnish with candied orange peel and basil leaves.   *Makes 6 servings*

classic chocolate chip cookies

1 ¼ cups all-purpose flour

½ teaspoon salt

½ teaspoon baking soda

½ cup (1 stick) dairy-free margarine, softened

½ cup granulated sugar

¼ cup packed brown sugar

1 egg, lightly beaten

1 teaspoon vanilla

1 cup dairy-free semisweet chocolate chips

½ cup coarsely chopped walnuts (optional)

1. Preheat oven to 350°F. Lightly grease cookie sheets. Combine flour, salt and baking soda in medium bowl.

2. Beat margarine, granulated sugar and brown sugar in large bowl with electric mixer at medium speed until light and fluffy. Add egg and vanilla; beat until well blended. Add flour mixture; beat just until blended. Stir in chocolate chips and walnuts, if desired.

3. Drop tablespoonfuls of dough 2 inches apart onto prepared cookie sheets.

4. Bake 10 to 12 minutes or until edges are lightly browned. Cool on cookie sheets 1 minute. Remove to wire racks; cool completely.

Makes about 3 dozen cookies

cranberry pound cake

1 ½ cups sugar
1 cup (2 sticks) dairy-free margarine, softened
¼ teaspoon ground nutmeg
4 eggs
½ teaspoon vanilla
2 cups cake flour
1 cup coarsely chopped cranberries

1. Preheat oven to 350°F. Grease and flour 9×5-inch loaf pan.

2. Beat sugar, margarine and nutmeg in large bowl with electric mixer at medium speed until light and fluffy. Beat in eggs, one at a time, until well blended. Beat in vanilla. Add flour ½ cup at a time, beating well at low speed after each addition. Fold in cranberries. Spoon batter into prepared pan.

3. Bake 60 to 70 minutes or until toothpick inserted into center comes out clean. Cool in pan on wire rack 5 minutes. Run knife around edges of pan to loosen cake; cool 30 minutes. Remove from pan; cool completely on wire rack.   *Makes 12 servings*

Tip: To easily chop cranberries, place them in a food processor and pulse two or three times.

date gingerbread

1¼ cups plus 1 teaspoon all-purpose flour, divided
¾ cup finely chopped pitted dates (about 18 whole dates)
½ cup whole wheat flour
¼ cup packed brown sugar
1 tablespoon finely chopped candied ginger
½ teaspoon baking powder
½ teaspoon baking soda
½ teaspoon ground ginger
½ teaspoon ground nutmeg
½ cup water
½ cup molasses
¼ cup canola or vegetable oil
2 egg whites
Whipped Coconut Cream Topping (page 101) or other dairy-free topping

1. Preheat oven to 350°F. Spray 8-inch round cake pan with nonstick cooking spray. Dust with 1 teaspoon all-purpose flour.

2. Combine remaining 1¼ cups all-purpose flour, dates, whole wheat flour, brown sugar, candied ginger, baking powder, baking soda, ground ginger and nutmeg in large bowl. Add water, molasses, oil and egg whites; beat with electric mixer at low speed until combined. Beat at high speed 2 minutes. Pour into prepared pan.

3. Bake 38 to 40 minutes or until toothpick inserted into center comes out clean. Cool in pan 10 minutes. Cut into wedges; serve warm. Garnish with Whipped Coconut Cream Topping. *Makes 8 servings*

peppermint brownies

½ cup (1 stick) dairy-free margarine, softened

4 squares (1 ounce each) unsweetened chocolate

2 cups sugar

4 eggs, beaten

½ teaspoon peppermint extract

1 cup all-purpose flour

1 cup coarsely chopped walnuts (optional)

½ cup finely crushed peppermint candies (18 candies)*

To crush, place unwrapped candy in heavy-duty resealable food storage bag. Loosely seal bag; crush candy with rolling pin, meat mallet or heavy skillet.

1. Preheat oven to 325°F. Grease 9-inch square baking pan.

2. Place margarine and chocolate in medium microwavable bowl. Microwave on HIGH 2 minutes. Stir until melted and smooth.** Cool slightly.

3. Whisk sugar and eggs in large bowl until blended. Add chocolate mixture and peppermint extract; mix well. Gradually stir in flour just until moistened. Fold in walnuts, if desired. Spread batter in prepared pan.

4. Bake 35 to 40 minutes or until edges begin to pull away from sides of pan. Immediately sprinkle with crushed candy. Cool completely in pan on wire rack. Cut into bars.   *Makes 12 brownies*

**Or melt margarine and chocolate in small saucepan over low heat, stirring until completely melted.*

Tip: For more cake-like brownies, use an 8-inch square baking pan.

espresso chocolate cheesecake

2 cups (10 ounces) dairy-free fudge brownie mix

¼ cup vegetable or canola oil

¼ cup water

3 eggs, divided

1 package (16 ounces) silken tofu, drained

2 packages (8 ounces each) dairy-free cream cheese alternative

1 cup sugar

½ cup unsweetened cocoa powder

4 teaspoons instant espresso granules, dissolved in 2 tablespoons boiling water

1 teaspoon vanilla

1 jar (10 ounces) raspberry fruit spread

Whipped Coconut Cream Topping (page 101) or other dairy-free topping

1. Preheat oven to 325°F. Grease 9-inch springform pan.

2. Combine brownie mix, oil, water and 1 egg in medium bowl; mix well. Pour batter into prepared pan. Bake 20 minutes or until toothpick inserted 2 inches from edge comes out clean. Cool in pan on wire rack.

3. Place tofu in food processor; process until smooth. Add dairy-free cream cheese and sugar; process until well blended. Add cocoa, remaining 2 eggs, espresso and vanilla; process until smooth.

4. Remove lid from fruit spread. Microwave on HIGH 30 seconds; stir. (Jar may be very hot.) Pour melted spread evenly over crust. Pour batter evenly over fruit spread.

5. Bake 45 minutes until edges are firm but center is still soft. Turn off oven and leave door slightly ajar for 1 hour. Cool completely and refrigerate before serving. *Makes 10 servings*

Contents

the basics of allergy-free cooking

What Is a Food Allergy?

The term "food allergy" means different things to different people. It can be a life-threatening condition, a mild sensitivity to a particular ingredient, or anything in between. By definition, a true allergy is one in which the body's immune system overreacts to a protein that is normally harmless. Symptoms can range from a rash to anaphylactic shock. Milk, egg and nut allergies are classic examples.

Food sensitivities or intolerances are often also called allergies, though they don't fit the same narrow definition. For example, many people are sensitive to the lactose in milk products and have trouble digesting it. Strictly speaking, they are lactose intolerant, not allergic to dairy. Those with celiac disease have an autoimmune condition caused by a reaction to the gluten in food. It is a serious, chronic condition, not a true allergy. Others choose to avoid certain foods because they feel better physically or mentally when they abstain.

Always have your doctor evaluate your allergies. Misinterpreting symptoms or self-diagnosing can be dangerous.

You Are Not Alone

It is estimated that more than 11 million people have food allergies and the number appears to be growing. According to the Centers for Disease Control and Prevention, the number of children allergic to foods has increased 18 percent in the last decade. There are many theories, but no proven

explanations for this increase. The good news is that a great deal of research is underway and awareness of the problem has increased everywhere from the doctor's office to the classroom.

Eating Well Without

Dietary restrictions can be an opportunity as well as a burden. Try new ethnic ingredients such as rice noodles or nutritious grains like quinoa. You'll find ideas to inspire you and recipes to delight you right here.

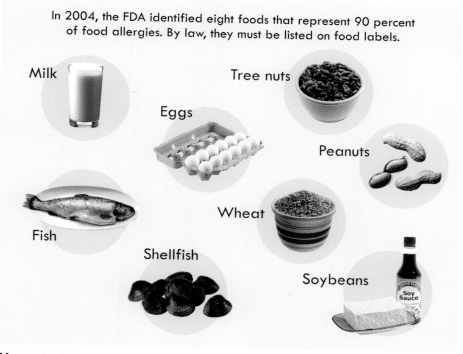

In 2004, the FDA identified eight foods that represent 90 percent of food allergies. By law, they must be listed on food labels.

Milk

Tree nuts

Eggs

Peanuts

Fish

Wheat

Shellfish

Soybeans

Note: *This book does not specifically label recipes that are free of fish or shellfish, though many recipes included do not contain these allergens.*

The Icons and Their Meaning

Recipes with this icon are gluten-free as well as wheat-free.

 Recipes with this icon are dairy-free (no milk, cheese, yogurt or other dairy).

Recipes with this icon contain no eggs or egg products.

 Recipes with this icon contain no tree nuts or peanuts.

 Recipes with this icon contain no soy.

Variations to the recipes are given when appropriate. For instance, if cheese or other dairy products can be eliminated, a dairy-free option is included under the main recipe.

egg allergies, unscrambled

Egg allergies usually occur in early childhood and more than half of those are outgrown by age seven. Of course, as with all allergies, there are exceptions. In some cases, the allergy remains lifelong or first surfaces in adolescence or adulthood. Both the yolk and the white of an egg contain proteins that can cause a reaction.

An Egg by Any Other Name

At first blush, avoiding eggs sounds simple. Just don't eat them poached, scrambled, fried or over easy! Unfortunately, eggs are present in many foods and hide under many names. Most baked goods use eggs for richness and lightness and the shiny crust on breads and pastries is created with an egg wash. Commercially made pancakes, waffles, donuts, crackers and pretzels usually contain eggs, as do many sauces and prepared entrées. Most food that is battered or breaded also contains egg, since it helps the coating stick. Pasta and noodles are often made with eggs, but there are some egg-free versions available.

Label Lingo

You probably know that you must avoid mayonnaise, meringue and custard. You may not know that there are some obscure ingredient names that are aliases for eggs. Any word beginning with the prefix "ovo" is suspicious. Albumin and globulin are also egg products. Always read labels carefully and check for the allergen statement, which legally must appear somewhere.

Baking without Cracking an Egg

In many baked goods requiring no more than three eggs, silken tofu is an acceptable replacement. (Use ¼ cup of tofu to replace each egg.) One mashed banana or ¼ cup of applesauce can often fill in for one egg in quick breads or muffins that are on the sweet side.

When Is an Egg Substitute NOT a Substitute?

Most cholesterol-free egg substitutes are made from egg whites. They were created to allow people to enjoy eggs without the cholesterol found in the yolks. There are a few egg-free replacement products, but check labels carefully. Look for one that specifies "vegan."

nut allergies in a nutshell

Tree Nuts and Peanuts

Both tree nuts and peanuts are considered together in this book, and recipes free from both are marked with the nut-free icon. You are probably aware that peanuts are legumes, not nuts. You may also know that many children and adults who are allergic to peanuts are also allergic to tree nuts and vice versa.

It's Nuts Not to Be Cautious

While very few reactions are severe, even a mild allergic response to nuts should be taken seriously. Future reactions can be more troublesome. Peanut allergies are responsible for more fatalities than any other food allergy. Even trace amounts can cause reactions.

Tree nuts include almonds, Brazil nuts, cashews, filberts (hazelnuts), macadamia nuts, pecans, pine nuts (pignoli), pistachios and walnuts. A person may be allergic to only one or two tree nuts, but it's best to avoid them all unless you are certain.

A Nut by Any Other Name

Nut proteins can be present in candies, cookies, crackers and other processed foods. Peanut oil is frequently used for cooking, especially in Asian and other ethnic recipes. Read labels carefully every time. Don't assume that ingredients haven't changed—they often do.

When Is a Nut Not a Nut?

When it's a water chestnut or a nutmeg. Neither is botanically related to tree nuts or peanuts, so they rarely present a problem. Coconut is a fruit and is usually not allergenic. However, the FDA recently reclassified it as a tree nut, so products that contain coconut now carry a warning. Pine nuts are also considered tree nuts, but are sometimes tolerated. Soy nuts are legumes, not nuts. Consult your doctor and when in doubt, don't!

Some Nutty Substitutions

Nuts used as a topping can easily be replaced with crushed potato chips, corn chips or toasted bread crumbs. Sunflower or pumpkin seeds can be excellent nut replacements, if they are tolerated. Sunflower seed butter or soy nut butter can stand in for peanut butter.

Better Breakfasts

ham and asparagus quiche

 gluten-free | nut-free | soy-free

2 cups sliced asparagus (½-inch pieces)
1 red bell pepper, chopped
1 cup milk
2 tablespoons rice flour
3 eggs
1 cup chopped cooked deli ham
2 tablespoons chopped fresh tarragon or basil
½ teaspoon salt
¼ teaspoon black pepper
½ cup (2 ounces) finely shredded Swiss cheese

1. Preheat oven to 350°F. Combine asparagus, bell pepper and 1 tablespoon water in microwavable bowl. Cover with waxed paper; microwave on HIGH 2 minutes or until vegetables are crisp-tender. Drain.

2. Whisk milk and rice flour in large bowl. Whisk in eggs until well blended. Stir in vegetables, ham, tarragon, salt and black pepper. Pour into 9-inch pie plate.

3. Bake 35 minutes. Sprinkle cheese over quiche; bake 5 minutes or until center is set and cheese is melted. Let stand 5 minutes before serving. Cut into 6 wedges. *Makes 6 servings*

 gluten-free | dairy-free | nut-free

Replace milk with unsweetened soymilk and omit Swiss cheese or use a dairy-free cheese alternative.

blueberry pancakes with blueberry-spice syrup

 dairy-free | nut-free

Blueberry-Spice Syrup (recipe follows)
1 cup all-purpose flour
2 tablespoons sugar
2 teaspoons baking powder
¼ teaspoon salt
¾ cup plain or vanilla soymilk
2 egg whites
1 tablespoon dairy-free margarine, melted
½ cup blueberries

1. Prepare Blueberry-Spice Syrup; set aside.

2. Combine flour, sugar, baking powder and salt in medium bowl. Beat soymilk and egg whites in small bowl; stir in margarine. Add soymilk mixture to flour mixture, stirring until almost smooth. Gently fold in blueberries.

3. Spray large nonstick skillet with cooking spray. Heat over medium heat until water droplets bounce off surface. Pour ¼ cupfuls of batter into skillet. Cook 2 to 3 minutes until bubbles appear at edges and bottoms of pancakes are lightly browned and edges begin to bubble. Turn over; cook until lightly browned. Serve with Blueberry-Spice Syrup.

Makes 4 servings

blueberry-spice syrup

  gluten-free | dairy-free | egg-free
nut-free | soy-free

½ cup blueberries, divided
½ cup maple syrup, divided
½ teaspoon grated lemon peel
½ teaspoon ground cinnamon
¼ teaspoon ground nutmeg

Bring ¼ cup blueberries and ¼ cup syrup to a boil in small saucepan over medium heat. Mash hot berries with fork. Add remaining ¼ cup blueberries and ¼ cup syrup, lemon peel, cinnamon and nutmeg. Cook and stir over medium heat about 2 minutes or until heated through.

veggie-beef hash

gluten-free | dairy-free | nut-free | soy-free

4 ounces cooked roast beef, finely chopped

1 ½ cups frozen seasoning blend*

1 cup shredded potatoes

½ cup shredded carrots

1 egg

½ teaspoon dried rosemary

½ teaspoon black pepper

Salsa (optional)

*Frozen seasoning blend is a combination of finely chopped onion, celery, green and red bell peppers and parsley flakes. Fresh sliced bell peppers and onion can be substituted.

1. Combine beef, seasoning blend, potatoes, carrots, egg, rosemary and black pepper in large bowl.

2. Spray large nonstick skillet with nonstick cooking spray; heat over medium-high heat. Spread beef mixture in skillet; flatten with spatula. Cook 4 minutes or until browned on bottom. Turn; cook 4 minutes or until lightly browned and heated through. Serve with salsa, if desired.

Makes 2 servings

Tip: Hash is an excellent way to turn last night's leftovers into a hot, hearty breakfast. Use whatever type of meat you have on hand—deli meat, leftover burgers or sausage—almost anything works. For a vegetarian version, replace the beef with tofu or more vegetables.

breakfast tacos

gluten-free I dairy-free I nut-free

6 mini taco shells *or* 2 regular taco shells
2 eggs
½ teaspoon gluten-free taco seasoning mix
2 tablespoons shredded dairy-free Cheddar cheese alternative
2 tablespoons salsa
2 tablespoons chopped fresh parsley
    Shredded lettuce

1. Heat taco shells according to package directions.

2. Meanwhile, beat eggs in small bowl until well blended. Spray small nonstick skillet with nonstick cooking spray; heat over medium-low heat. Pour eggs into skillet; cook and stir until desired doneness. Sprinkle with taco seasoning.

3. Spoon eggs into taco shells. Top with dairy-free cheese, salsa, parsley and lettuce.   *Makes 2 servings*

scrambled tofu and potatoes

gluten-free | dairy-free | egg-free | nut-free

Potatoes

¼ cup plus 2 tablespoons olive oil, divided

4 to 5 red potatoes, cubed

½ white onion, sliced

1 tablespoon chopped fresh rosemary

1 teaspoon coarse salt

Scrambled Tofu

¼ cup nutritional yeast

½ teaspoon turmeric

2 tablespoons water

2 tablespoons gluten-free soy sauce

1 package (14 ounces) firm tofu

1 tablespoon vegetable oil

½ cup chopped green bell pepper

½ cup chopped red onion

2 green onions, chopped

1. For potatoes, preheat oven to 450°F. Place ¼ cup olive oil in 12-inch cast-iron skillet; place skillet in oven 10 minutes to heat.

2. Combine potatoes, onion, remaining 2 tablespoons olive oil, rosemary and salt in large bowl. Spread in preheated skillet. Bake 25 to 30 minutes or until potatoes are browned and tender, stirring every 10 minutes.

3. For tofu, combine nutritional yeast and turmeric in small bowl; stir in water and soy sauce until smooth.

4. Cut tofu into 8 cubes. Gently squeeze out water; loosely crumble tofu into medium bowl. Heat 1 tablespoon oil in large skillet over medium-high heat. Add green pepper and red onion; cook and stir 2 minutes or until soft but not browned. Add tofu; drizzle with 3 tablespoons nutritional yeast sauce. Cook and stir about 5 minutes or until liquid is evaporated and tofu is uniformly colored and heated through. Stir in additional sauce, if desired, for stronger flavor.

5. Divide potatoes among four serving plates. Top with tofu and sprinkle with green onions.   *Makes 4 servings*

breakfast quinoa

gluten-free I dairy-free I egg-free
nut-free I soy-free

½ cup uncooked quinoa

1 cup water

1 tablespoon packed brown sugar

2 teaspoons maple syrup

½ teaspoon ground cinnamon

¼ cup golden raisins (optional)

Raspberries and banana slices

1. Place quinoa in fine-mesh strainer; rinse well under cold running water. Transfer to small saucepan. Stir in water, brown sugar, maple syrup and cinnamon. Bring to a boil. Reduce heat; cover and simmer 10 to 15 minutes or until water is absorbed and quinoa is tender. Add raisins, if desired, during last 5 minutes of cooking.

2. Top quinoa with raspberries and bananas.   *Makes 2 servings*

summer fruit brunch cake

 gluten-free I dairy-free

¾ cup Gluten-Free All-Purpose Flour Blend (page 5)*
½ cup cornmeal
1 teaspoon xanthan gum
½ teaspoon baking powder
¼ teaspoon baking soda
⅔ cup sugar
½ cup (1 stick) dairy-free margarine, softened
2 eggs
½ cup vanilla soy yogurt, plus additional for topping
1 cup fresh peach slices or 1 can (about 15 ounces) sliced peaches in juice, drained
Sliced strawberries

*Or use any gluten-free all-purpose flour blend that does not contain xanthan gum.

1. Preheat oven to 325°F. Spray 9-inch pie plate with nonstick cooking spray. Combine flour blend, cornmeal, xanthan gum, baking powder and baking soda in medium bowl.

2. Beat sugar and margarine in large bowl with electric mixer at medium speed until fluffy. Add eggs and ½ cup yogurt; beat until well blended. Beat in flour mixture until combined. Stir in peaches. Pour batter into prepared pie plate.

3. Bake 35 minutes or until toothpick inserted into center comes out clean. Serve with strawberries and drizzle with additional yogurt.

Makes 6 servings

breakfast pizza

 gluten-free | nut-free

2 cups refrigerated or frozen shredded hash brown potatoes, thawed

½ cup finely chopped onion

¼ cup tomato paste

2 tablespoons water

½ teaspoon dried oregano

2 eggs, beaten

½ cup (2 ounces) shredded mozzarella cheese

2 tablespoons bacon bits

1. Combine potatoes and onion in medium bowl.

2. Spray medium nonstick skillet with nonstick cooking spray. Add potato mixture; flatten with spatula. Cook 7 to 9 minutes on each side or until both sides are lightly browned.

3. Mix tomato paste and water in small bowl; spread evenly over potatoes in skillet. Sprinkle with oregano.

4. Pour eggs over potato mixture; cover and cook 4 minutes. Sprinkle mozzarella and bacon bits over egg; cover and cook 1 minute.

5. Slide pizza from skillet onto serving plate. Cut into 4 wedges.

Makes 2 to 4 servings

 gluten-free | dairy-free | nut-free

Omit cheese. Instead, top with cooked vegetables or a dairy-free cheese alternative.

breakfast rice pudding

gluten-free | dairy-free | egg-free | nut-free

2 cups vanilla soymilk, divided

¾ cup brown rice*

⅓ cup packed brown sugar

½ teaspoon ground cinnamon

½ teaspoon salt

¼ cup golden raisins or dried sweetened cranberries (optional)

½ teaspoon vanilla

Mixed berries (optional)

Look for rice that cooks in 20 to 25 minutes. For rice with a longer cooking time, increase the cooking time in step 1.

1. Bring 1½ cups soymilk to a boil in medium saucepan. Stir in rice, brown sugar, cinnamon and salt. Return to a boil. Reduce heat; cover and simmer 15 minutes.

2. Stir in remaining ½ cup soymilk and raisins, if desired. Cover and simmer 10 to 15 minutes or until rice is tender. Remove from heat; stir in vanilla. Serve with berries, if desired.   *Makes 4 servings*

Note: Rice thickens as it cools. For a thinner consistency, stir in additional soymilk just before serving.

Tip: Rice for breakfast is traditional in most Asian cultures and makes a great start to anyone's day. Brown rice is more nutritious and flavorful than ordinary white rice, though it does take longer to cook. When you're preparing rice, make a big batch. You can easily freeze leftover cooked rice for later use. After it cools in the refrigerator, pack 1- or 2-cup portions in resealable freezer food storage bags. Press out as much air as possible, label and freeze them. Rice thaws easily in the microwave or a steamer.

Light Bites

vegetable-topped hummus

dairy-free | egg-free | nut-free | soy-free

- 1 can (about 15 ounces) chickpeas, rinsed and drained
- 2 tablespoons tahini
- 2 tablespoons lemon juice
- 1 clove garlic
- 3/4 teaspoon salt
- 1 tomato, finely chopped
- 2 green onions, finely chopped
- 2 tablespoons chopped fresh parsley
- Pita chips or dairy-free pita bread

1. Combine chickpeas, tahini, lemon juice, garlic and salt in food processor or blender; process until smooth.

2. Combine tomato, green onions and parsley in small bowl; gently toss to combine.

3. Spoon hummus into serving bowl; top with tomato mixture. Serve with pita bread or assorted vegetables, if desired. *Makes 8 servings*

gluten-free | dairy-free | egg-free
nut-free | soy-free

Serve hummus with carrot and celery sticks, bell pepper strips and cucumber slices.

sweet potato gnocchi

gluten-free | dairy-free | egg-free
nut-free | soy-free

1½ pounds sweet potatoes (2 or 3 medium)
¼ cup sweet rice flour,* plus additional for rolling
1 tablespoon lemon juice
1 teaspoon salt
½ teaspoon xanthan gum
½ teaspoon ground nutmeg
½ teaspoon black pepper
¼ teaspoon sugar
2 to 4 tablespoons extra virgin olive oil
1 pound spinach, stemmed

*Sweet rice flour is usually labeled mochiko (the Japanese term).

1. Preheat oven to 350°F. Bake sweet potatoes 1 hour or until tender. Or pierce sweet potatoes several times with fork and place on microwavable plate. Microwave on HIGH 16 to 18 minutes, rotating halfway through cooking time. Let stand 5 minutes.

2. Cut hot sweet potatoes lengthwise into halves. Scrape pulp from skins into medium bowl. Add rice flour, lemon juice, salt, xanthan gum, nutmeg, pepper and sugar; mix well.

3. Heavily dust cutting board or work surface with rice flour. Working in batches, scoop portions of dough onto board and roll into ½-inch-thick rope using rice-floured hands. Cut each rope into ¾-inch pieces. Press against tines of fork to make ridges. Freeze gnocchi at least 30 minutes on baking sheet.*

4. Heat 1 tablespoon oil in large nonstick skillet. Add gnocchi in single layer and cook, turning once, until lightly browned and heated through, adding additional oil as needed to prevent sticking. Keep warm.

5. Add remaining 1 tablespoon oil to skillet. Add spinach; cook and stir 30 seconds or until barely wilted. Serve with gnocchi.

Makes 4 servings (about 40 gnocchi)

Gnocchi may be made ahead to this point and frozen for up to 24 hours. For longer storage, transfer frozen gnocchi to airtight freezer container.

chicken tortilla soup

gluten-free | dairy-free | egg-free
nut-free | soy-free

       2 tablespoons canola oil
     ½ cup finely chopped onion
     ½ cup finely chopped carrot
2½ cups shredded cooked rotisserie chicken
       1 cup thick and chunky salsa
       4 cups gluten-free chicken broth
       1 tablespoon lime juice
       1 avocado, chopped
     10 corn tortilla chips, broken into thirds

1. Heat oil in large saucepan over high heat. Add onion and carrot; cook and stir 3 minutes or until onion is translucent.

2. Stir in chicken and salsa. Add broth; bring to a boil. Reduce heat to medium-low; cover and simmer 5 minutes or until carrot is crisp-tender. Remove from heat; stir in lime juice.

3. Top with avocado and tortilla chips before serving.

Makes 5 servings

Tip: Most tortilla chips are gluten- and soy-free, but always check ingredients lists and don't assume that a product remains free of allergens because it used to be. Recipes can change.

mushroom gratin

dairy-free | egg-free | nut-free

4 tablespoons dairy-free margarine, divided
1 small onion, minced
8 ounces (about 2½ cups) sliced cremini mushrooms
2 cloves garlic, minced
2 tablespoons all-purpose flour
1 cup unsweetened soymilk
½ teaspoon salt
½ teaspoon black pepper
½ teaspoon dry mustard
4 cups cooked elbow macaroni, rotini or other pasta
½ cup fresh bread crumbs
1 tablespoon extra virgin olive oil

1. Preheat oven to 350°F. Melt 2 tablespoons margarine in large skillet over medium-high heat. Add onion; cook and stir 2 minutes. Add mushrooms and garlic; cook and stir 6 to 8 minutes or until vegetables soften.

2. Melt remaining 2 tablespoons margarine in medium saucepan over low heat. Whisk in flour; cook and stir 2 minutes without browning. Stir in soymilk. Bring to a boil over medium-high heat, whisking constantly. Reduce heat to maintain a simmer. Add salt, pepper and mustard; whisk 5 to 7 minutes or until sauce thickens. Add pasta to mushroom mixture in skillet; stir in white sauce.

3. Spoon mixture into shallow baking dish or casserole. Top with bread crumbs and drizzle with oil. Cover and bake 15 minutes. Uncover and bake 10 minutes or until bubbly and browned.   *Makes 8 servings*

socca (niçoise chickpea pancake)

gluten-free | dairy-free | egg-free
nut-free | soy-free

1 cup chickpea flour
¾ teaspoon salt
½ teaspoon ground black pepper
1 cup water
5 tablespoons olive oil, divided
1½ teaspoons minced fresh basil *or* ½ teaspoon dried basil
1 teaspoon minced fresh rosemary *or* ¼ teaspoon dried rosemary
¼ teaspoon dried thyme

1. Sift chickpea flour into medium bowl. Stir in salt and pepper. Gradually whisk in water until smooth. Stir in 2 tablespoons oil. Let stand at least 30 minutes.

2. Preheat oven to 450°F. Place 9- or 10-inch cast iron skillet in oven to heat.

3. Add basil, rosemary and thyme to batter; whisk until smooth. Carefully remove skillet from oven. Add 2 tablespoons oil to skillet, swirling to coat pan evenly. Immediately pour in batter.

4. Bake 12 to 15 minutes or until edge of pancake begins to pull away from side of pan and center is firm. Remove from oven. Preheat broiler.

5. Brush with remaining 1 tablespoon oil. Broil 2 to 4 minutes or until dark brown in spots. Cut into wedges. Serve warm.   *Makes 6 servings*

Tip: Socca are pancakes made of chickpea flour and are commonly served in paper cones as a savory street food in the south of France, especially around Nice.

Note: Chickpea flour can also be used to make a thinner batter and cooked in a skillet to make a softer crêpe. Just increase the amount of water in the recipe by about ¼ cup.

greek salad with dairy-free feta

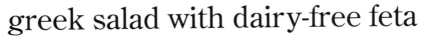 gluten-free | dairy-free | egg-free | nut-free

Dairy-Free Feta

- 1 package (about 14 ounces) firm or extra firm tofu
- ½ cup extra virgin olive oil
- ¼ cup lemon juice
- 2 teaspoons salt
- 2 teaspoons Greek or Italian seasoning
- ½ teaspoon black pepper
- 1 teaspoon onion powder
- ½ teaspoon garlic powder

Salad

- 1 pint grape tomatoes, halved
- 2 seedless cucumbers, sliced and quartered
- 1 yellow bell pepper, slivered
- 1 small red onion, cut in thin slices

1. Cut tofu crosswise into 2 pieces, each about 1 inch thick. Place on cutting board lined with paper towels; top with layer of paper towels. Place weighted baking dish on top of tofu. Let stand 30 minutes to drain. Pat tofu dry and crumble into large bowl.

2. Combine oil, lemon juice, salt, Greek seasoning and black pepper in small jar with lid; shake to combine well. Reserve ¼ cup mixture for salad dressing. Add onion powder and garlic powder to remaining mixture; pour over tofu and toss gently. Refrigerate 2 hours or overnight.

3. Combine tomatoes, cucumbers, bell pepper and onion in serving bowl. Add tofu and reserved dressing. Toss gently.   *Makes 4 to 6 servings*

falafel nuggets

gluten-free I dairy-free I nut-free I soy-free

Sauce

- 2½ cups gluten-free tomato sauce
- ⅓ cup tomato paste
- 2 tablespoons lemon juice
- 2 teaspoons sugar
- 1 teaspoon onion powder
- ½ teaspoon salt

Falafel

- 2 cans (about 15 ounces each) chickpeas, rinsed and drained
- ½ cup rice flour
- ½ cup chopped fresh parsley
- 1 egg
- ¼ cup minced onion
- 3 tablespoons lemon juice
- 2 tablespoons minced garlic
- 2 teaspoons ground cumin
- ½ teaspoon salt
- ½ teaspoon ground red pepper or red pepper flakes
- ½ cup canola oil

1. For sauce, combine tomato sauce, tomato paste, 2 tablespoons lemon juice, sugar, onion powder and ½ teaspoon salt in medium saucepan. Simmer over medium-low heat 20 minutes or until heated through. Cover and keep warm until ready to serve.

2. Meanwhile, preheat oven to 400°F. Spray baking sheet with nonstick cooking spray.

3. For falafel, combine chickpeas, rice flour, parsley, egg, minced onion, 3 tablespoons lemon juice, garlic, cumin, ½ teaspoon salt and red pepper in food processor or blender; process until well blended. Shape mixture into 1-inch balls.

4. Heat oil in large nonstick skillet over medium-high heat. Fry falafel in batches until browned. Using slotted spoon, remove from skillet and place 2 inches apart on prepared baking sheet.

5. Bake 8 to 10 minutes. Serve with warm sauce for dipping.

Makes 12 servings

Tip: Falafel can also be baked completely. Spray lightly with nonstick cooking spray and bake 15 to 20 minutes, turning once.

mediterranean vegetable bake

 gluten-free | dairy-free | egg-free
nut-free | soy-free

2 tomatoes, sliced

1 small red onion, sliced

1 medium zucchini, sliced

1 small eggplant, sliced

1 small yellow squash, sliced

1 large portobello mushroom, sliced

2 cloves garlic, finely chopped

3 tablespoons olive oil

2 teaspoons chopped fresh rosemary leaves

⅔ cup dry white wine

Salt and black pepper

1. Preheat oven to 350°F. Spray bottom of oval casserole or 13×9-inch baking dish with nonstick cooking spray.

2. Arrange vegetable slices in rows, alternating different types and overlapping slices to make attractive arrangement; sprinkle evenly with garlic. Combine olive oil and rosemary in small bowl; drizzle over vegetables.

3. Pour wine over vegetables; season with salt and pepper. Cover loosely with foil. Bake 20 minutes. Uncover; bake 10 to 15 minutes or until vegetables are tender. *Makes 4 to 6 servings*

Tip: Use any vegetables you have on hand or in your garden.

tuna tabbouleh salad

 dairy-free | egg-free | nut-free | soy-free

1 cup water
¾ cup uncooked fine-grain bulgur wheat
1 teaspoon grated lemon peel
3 tablespoons lemon juice
1 clove garlic, minced
½ teaspoon salt
⅛ teaspoon black pepper
3 tablespoons olive oil
1 cup red or yellow cherry tomatoes, quartered if large
1 cup chopped cucumber
¼ cup finely chopped red onion
3 cans (5 ounces each) chunk white albacore tuna packed in water, drained and flaked
½ cup chopped Italian parsley
Watercress

1. Bring water to a boil in small saucepan. Remove from heat and add bulgur; cover and let stand 15 minutes. Place bulgur in fine-mesh strainer; run under cold water to cool. Drain well.

2. Whisk lemon peel, lemon juice, garlic, salt and pepper in large bowl. Slowly whisk in olive oil. Add tomatoes, cucumber, onion and bulgur; stir to combine. Gently stir in tuna and parsley. Serve over watercress.

Makes 4 servings

gluten-free | dairy-free | egg-free
nut-free | soy-free

Omit bulgur wheat. Instead, use 1 cup quinoa cooked according to package directions.

Kid Stuff

chili con corny

gluten-free | egg-free | nut-free | soy-free

  1 tablespoon vegetable oil
  ½ cup finely chopped onion
  1 pound ground turkey
  1 can (about 15 ounces) kidney beans, rinsed and drained
  1 can (about 14 ounces) diced tomatoes
  1 can (11 ounces) corn, drained
  1 can (8 ounces) gluten-free tomato sauce
  2 teaspoons chili powder
  1 teaspoon salt
  1 teaspoon ground cumin
  ¾ cup (3 ounces) shredded Cheddar cheese
  2 cups corn chips

1. Heat oil in large skillet over medium heat. Add onion; cook and stir 2 minutes. Add turkey; cook until no longer pink, stirring to break up meat.

2. Stir in beans, tomatoes, corn, tomato sauce, chili powder, salt and cumin. Bring mixture to a simmer; cook 10 minutes, stirring frequently.

3. Serve chili topped with cheese and corn chips. *Makes 4 servings*

gluten-free | dairy-free | egg-free | nut-free

Omit the Cheddar cheese or substitute dairy-free cheese alternative.

yam yums

gluten-free | egg-free | nut-free | soy-free

2 large unpeeled sweet potatoes, scrubbed

¼ cup maple syrup (not pancake syrup)

2 tablespoons orange juice

2 tablespoons butter, melted

⅛ teaspoon ground nutmeg

Salt and black pepper

1. Preheat oven to 350°F. Line baking sheet with foil.

2. Cut sweet potatoes crosswise into ½-inch-thick slices; place on cutting board. Cut shapes and letters from slices with small metal cookie cutters (1½ inches in diameter) or sharp knife.

3. Combine maple syrup, orange juice and butter in small bowl. Arrange potato shapes in single layer on prepared baking sheet. Season both sides with nutmeg, salt and pepper. Brush both sides generously with maple syrup mixture.

4. Bake 20 to 30 minutes or until tender, turning once and basting with remaining syrup mixture. *Makes about 4 servings*

 gluten-free | dairy-free | egg-free
nut-free | soy-free

Replace butter with dairy-free soy-free margarine.

flourless fried chicken tenders

gluten-free I nut-free I soy-free

1 ½ cups chickpea flour*
1 ½ teaspoons Italian seasoning
1 teaspoon salt
½ teaspoon black pepper
⅛ teaspoon ground red pepper
¾ cup plus 2 to 4 tablespoons water
  Curry Mayo Dipping Sauce (recipe follows, optional)
  Vegetable oil
1 pound chicken tenders, cut in half if large

*Chickpea flour is also called garbanzo flour. It is found in the specialty food section of most supermarkets.

1. Sift chickpea flour into medium bowl. Stir in Italian seasoning, salt, black pepper and red pepper. Gradually whisk in ¾ cup water until smooth. Whisk in additional water by tablespoonfuls until batter is consistency of heavy cream.

2. Prepare Curry Mayo Dipping Sauce, if desired. Add 1 inch oil to large heavy skillet or Dutch oven. Heat over medium-high heat until oil registers 350°F on deep-fry thermometer or drop of batter placed in oil sizzles.

3. Pat chicken pieces dry. Dip chicken into batter with tongs; let excess drip back into bowl. Slide chicken gently into oil in batches. (Do not crowd pan.) Fry 2 to 3 minutes on each side or until slightly browned and chicken is cooked through.

4. Drain chicken on paper towels. Serve warm with dipping sauce.

Makes 4 servings

Curry Mayo Dipping Sauce: Combine ½ cup mayonnaise, ¼ cup sour cream and ½ teaspoon curry powder in small bowl. Stir in 2 tablespoons minced fresh cilantro.

gluten-free I dairy-free I egg-free
nut-free I soy-free

Serve the chicken with salsa or Dairy-Free Ranch Dressing (page 136).

kids' oasis

 dairy-free | egg-free | nut-free | soy-free

2 cans (about 15 ounces each) chickpeas, rinsed and drained

¼ cup tahini

Juice of 1 lemon

1 tablespoon olive oil, plus additional for serving

3 cloves garlic, minced

½ teaspoon salt

¼ teaspoon ground black pepper

2 cups broccoli florets

1 box (10 ounces) plain couscous, plus ingredients to prepare couscous

Green onions and chives (optional)

1. For hummus, place chickpeas, tahini, lemon juice, oil, garlic, salt and pepper in food processor; process 2 to 3 minutes or until smooth.

2. Cook broccoli in boiling salted water until crisp-tender; drain. Prepare couscous according to package directions.

3. For each oasis, spread ¼ cup hummus in center of plate. Insert broccoli "trees" and surround with couscous "sand." Drizzle with additional olive oil and garnish with green onions and chives, if desired.

Makes 12 servings

gluten-free | dairy-free | egg-free
nut-free | soy-free

Serve hummus with quinoa or polenta instead of couscous.

mini s'mores pies

dairy-free | egg-free | nut-free

    6 mini graham cracker pie crusts
    ½ cup dairy-free semisweet chocolate chips, divided
    ¾ cup mini marshmallows

1. Preheat oven to 325°F. Place pie crusts on baking sheet.

2. Divide ¼ cup chocolate chips among pie crusts. Sprinkle marshmallows over chocolate chips. Top with remaining ¼ cup chocolate chips.

3. Bake 3 to 5 minutes or until marshmallows are light golden brown.

Makes 6 servings

tickle sticks

gluten-free | egg-free | nut-free | soy-free

    1 pound watermelon
    1 container (6 ounces) plain yogurt
    2 teaspoons honey
      Grated peel and juice of 1 lime

1. Cut watermelon into sticks about 3 inches long and ½ inch wide. Remove and discard seeds.

2. Combine yogurt, honey, lime peel and lime juice in small bowl. Serve with watermelon sticks.

Makes 4 to 6 servings

gluten-free | dairy-free | egg-free | nut-free

Substitute plain or vanilla soy yogurt for regular yogurt.

allergy-free birthday cake

gluten-free | dairy-free | egg-free

3 cups Gluten-Free All-Purpose Flour Blend (page 5),* plus
   additional for pans

2 cups sugar

6 tablespoons unsweetened cocoa powder

2 teaspoons baking soda

2 teaspoons xanthan gum

1 teaspoon salt

2 cups chocolate soymilk

½ cup plus 2 tablespoons vegetable oil

2 tablespoons cider vinegar

1 teaspoon vanilla

   Chocolate No-Butter Buttercream Frosting (page 243)

Or use any all-purpose gluten-free flour blend that does not contain xanthan gum.

1. Preheat oven to 350°F. Grease and flour two 9-inch round cake pans.

2. Whisk flour blend, sugar, cocoa, baking soda, xanthan gum and salt in large bowl. Combine soymilk, oil, vinegar and vanilla in small bowl.

3. Pour wet ingredients into dry; stir until smooth, scraping bottom and side of bowl. Immediately pour into prepared pans and place in oven.

4. Bake 25 to 30 minutes or until toothpick inserted into centers comes out clean. (Middle of cake may look darker than edges.) Cool in pans 5 minutes. Carefully invert onto wire racks; cool completely.

5. Meanwhile, prepare Chocolate No-Butter Buttercream Frosting. Fill and frost cake. Decorate as desired. *Makes 10 servings*

dairy-free | egg-free | nut-free

Replace gluten-free all-purpose flour blend with regular all-purpose flour. Omit xanthan gum. Proceed as directed.

chocolate no-butter buttercream frosting

 gluten-free | dairy-free | egg-free | nut-free

- ¾ cup (1½ sticks) dairy-free margarine
- 2 teaspoons vanilla
- 4 cups powdered sugar
- ½ cup unsweetened cocoa powder
- 4 to 6 tablespoons soy creamer

1. Beat margarine in large bowl with electric mixer at medium speed until light and fluffy. Beat in vanilla.

2. Gradually beat in powdered sugar and cocoa. Beat in soy creamer 1 tablespoon at a time until spreadable.

scrambled egg & zucchini pie

gluten-free | nut-free | soy-free

2 teaspoons butter

1 small zucchini, chopped

2 eggs

2 tablespoons grated Parmesan or Cheddar cheese

¼ teaspoon salt

1. Preheat oven to 350°F. Melt butter in small nonstick ovenproof skillet over medium-high heat. Add zucchini; cook and stir 2 to 3 minutes or until crisp-tender.

2. Meanwhile, beat eggs in small bowl; stir in cheese and salt.

3. Reduce heat to low; stir egg mixture into skillet with zucchini. Cook without stirring 4 to 5 minutes or until eggs begin to set around edge.

4. Transfer skillet to oven and bake 5 minutes or until eggs are set. Cut into wedges to serve. *Makes 4 to 6 servings*

gluten-free | dairy-free | nut-free

Substitute dairy-free margarine for the butter and vegan Parmesan-flavor topping for the Parmesan cheese.

magic rainbow pops

gluten-free | egg-free | nut-free | soy-free

1 envelope (¼ ounce) unflavored gelatin
¼ cup cold water
½ cup boiling water
1 container (6 ounces) raspberry or strawberry yogurt
1 container (6 ounces) lemon or orange yogurt
1 can (8¼ ounces) apricots or peaches with juice

1. Combine gelatin and cold water in 2-cup glass measuring cup. Let stand 5 minutes to soften. Stir in boiling water until gelatin is completely dissolved. Cool.

2. For first layer, combine raspberry yogurt and ¼ cup gelatin mixture in small bowl; stir until completely blended. Fill each pop mold about one third full with raspberry mixture. Freeze 30 to 60 minutes or until set.

3. For second layer, combine lemon yogurt and ¼ cup gelatin mixture in small bowl; stir until completely blended. Pour lemon mixture over raspberry layer in each mold. Freeze 30 to 60 minutes or until set.

4. For third layer, combine apricots with juice and remaining ¼ cup gelatin mixture in blender or food processor; blend until smooth. Pour mixture over lemon layer in each mold. Cover with lids. Freeze 2 to 5 hours or until firm.*

5. To remove pops from molds, place bottoms of pops under warm running water until loosened. Press firmly on bottoms to release. (Do not twist or pull lids.)   *Makes about 6 pops*

If you aren't using pop molds with lids, cover each pop with small piece of foil and insert sticks through center of foil.

Tip: Three-ounce paper or plastic cups can be used in place of the molds. Cover each cup with small piece of foil and freeze 1 hour before inserting sticks. Freeze until firm. To serve, remove foil and peel away paper cups or gently twist frozen pops out of plastic cups.

gluten-free | dairy-free | egg-free | nut-free

Replace the regular yogurt with dairy-free soy or rice yogurt.

Main Events

spanish chicken with rice

 gluten-free | dairy-free | egg-free
nut-free | soy-free

  2 tablespoons olive oil
10 ounces cooked pork sausage, sliced into ½-inch rounds
  6 boneless skinless chicken thighs (about 1 pound)
  1 onion, diced
  5 cloves garlic, minced
  2 cups long grain white rice
  1 red bell pepper, chopped
  ½ cup diced carrots
  ½ teaspoon salt
  ¼ teaspoon black pepper
  ¼ teaspoon saffron threads, crushed
3½ cups hot gluten-free chicken broth
  ½ cup peas

Slow Cooker Directions

1. Heat oil in medium skillet over medium heat. Add sausage; cook and stir until browned. Transfer to slow cooker with slotted spoon.

2. Add chicken to skillet and brown on all sides. Transfer to slow cooker. Add onion to skillet; cook and stir until soft. Stir in garlic; cook 30 seconds. Transfer to slow cooker.

3. Add rice, bell pepper, carrots, salt, black pepper and saffron, if desired. Pour in broth. Cover; cook on HIGH 3½ to 4 hours.

4. Stir in peas; cook 15 minutes or until heated through.

Makes 6 servings

beef stew stroganoff

gluten-free | egg-free | nut-free | soy-free

2 tablespoons olive oil or canola oil
1 ½ pounds lean boneless beef (bottom round), cut into 1-inch cubes
1 teaspoon caraway seeds
½ teaspoon salt
½ teaspoon black pepper
½ teaspoon dried thyme
2 cans (about 14 ounces each) gluten-free beef broth
1 cup sliced mushrooms
½ cup thinly sliced carrots
½ cup chopped red bell pepper
6 ounces baby red potatoes, unpeeled, quartered (about 6 small)
¼ cup sour cream

1. Heat oil in large saucepan over medium-high heat. Add beef; cook and stir until meat juices evaporate and begin to caramelize. Add caraway seeds, salt, black pepper and thyme. Pour in broth, stirring to scrape up browned bits. Bring to a boil.

2. Add mushrooms, carrots and bell pepper. Reduce heat to low; cover and simmer 1 hour.

3. Add potatoes; bring to a boil. Reduce heat to low; cover and simmer 20 minutes.

4. Stir in sour cream; cook 2 minutes or until heated through.

Makes 6 servings

gluten-free | dairy-free | egg-free | nut-free

Substitute dairy-free sour cream or soy yogurt for the regular sour cream.

sesame ginger-glazed tofu with rice

gluten-free | dairy-free | egg-free | nut-free

1 package (14 ounces) extra firm tofu
1 cup sesame ginger stir-fry sauce, divided
1 cup uncooked long grain rice
4 medium carrots, chopped (about 1 cup)
4 ounces snow peas, halved (about 1 cup)

1. Slice tofu in half crosswise. Cut each half into 2 triangles. Place tofu triangles on cutting board between layers of paper towels. Top with weighted baking dish. Let stand about 15 minutes.

2. Spread ½ cup stir-fry sauce in baking dish. Place tofu in sauce; marinate at room temperature 30 minutes, turning after 15 minutes.

3. Meanwhile, cook rice according to package directions. Keep warm.

4. Spray indoor grill pan with nonstick cooking spray; heat over medium-high heat. Grill tofu 6 to 8 minutes or until lightly browned, turning once.

5. Meanwhile, pour remaining ½ cup stir-fry sauce into large nonstick skillet; heat over medium-high heat. Add carrots and snow peas; cook and stir 4 to 6 minutes or until crisp-tender. Add rice; stir to combine. Serve with tofu.

Makes 4 servings

basil chicken with rice noodles

gluten-free I dairy-free I egg-free I nut-free

1 pound boneless skinless chicken breasts, cut into bite-size pieces

5 tablespoons gluten-free soy sauce, divided

1 tablespoon white wine or rice wine

3 cloves garlic, minced

1 tablespoon grated fresh ginger

8 ounces uncooked rice noodles

Juice of 2 limes

2 tablespoons packed brown sugar

1 tablespoon vegetable oil

1 red onion, sliced

1 yellow or red bell pepper, cut into strips

2 medium carrots, cut into matchstick-size pieces

2 jalapeño or serrano peppers,* seeded and chopped

1 ½ cups loosely packed basil leaves, shredded

Jalapeño peppers can sting and irritate the skin, so wear rubber gloves when handling peppers and do not touch your eyes.

1. Place chicken in shallow dish. Combine 3 tablespoons soy sauce, wine, garlic and ginger in small bowl. Pour over chicken and stir to coat. Marinate at room temperature 30 minutes or refrigerate up to 2 hours.

2. Place rice noodles in medium bowl. Cover with hot water; let stand 15 minutes or until tender. Drain.

3. Whisk remaining 2 tablespoons soy sauce, lime juice and brown sugar in small bowl until sugar is dissolved.

4. Heat oil in large skillet or wok over medium-high heat. Add chicken with marinade; cook and stir 5 minutes or until cooked through. Add onion, bell pepper, carrots and jalapeño peppers; cook and stir 4 to 6 minutes or until vegetables are crisp-tender.

5. Stir sauce and add to skillet; cook and stir 2 minutes. Add rice noodles and basil; toss to combine.   *Makes 4 to 6 servings*

midweek moussaka

gluten-free | egg-free | nut-free | soy-free

1 eggplant (about 1 pound), cut into ¼-inch slices
2 tablespoons olive oil
1 pound ground beef
1 can (about 14 ounces) stewed tomatoes, drained
¼ cup red wine
2 tablespoons tomato paste
2 teaspoons sugar
¾ teaspoon salt
½ teaspoon dried oregano
¼ teaspoon ground cinnamon
¼ teaspoon black pepper
⅛ teaspoon ground allspice
4 ounces cream cheese
¼ cup milk
¼ cup grated Parmesan cheese

1. Preheat broiler. Spray 8-inch baking dish with nonstick cooking spray.

2. Line baking sheet with foil. Arrange eggplant slices on foil; brush with oil. Broil 5 inches from heat 4 minutes on each side or until tender. *Reduce oven temperature to 350°F.*

3. Meanwhile, brown beef in large nonstick skillet over medium-high heat 6 to 8 minutes, stirring to break up meat. Drain fat. Add tomatoes, wine, tomato paste, sugar, salt, oregano, cinnamon, pepper and allspice. Bring to a boil, breaking up large pieces of tomato with spoon. Reduce heat to medium-low; cover and simmer 10 minutes.

4. Place cream cheese and milk in small microwavable bowl. Cover and microwave on HIGH 1 minute. Stir with fork until smooth.

5. Arrange half of eggplant slices in prepared baking dish. Top with half of meat sauce; sprinkle with half of Parmesan cheese. Repeat layers. Top evenly with cream cheese mixture. Bake 20 minutes or until top begins to crack slightly. Let stand 10 minutes before serving.   *Makes 4 servings*

pork with apples, fennel and cabbage

gluten-free | dairy-free | egg-free
nut-free | soy-free

1 ⅓ cup apple juice, divided

2 tablespoons balsamic vinegar

½ teaspoon caraway seeds

½ teaspoon dried thyme

4 boneless pork chops (about ¾ pound total)

¼ teaspoon salt

¼ teaspoon pepper

1 tablespoon canola oil

3 cups sliced green cabbage

1 medium bulb fennel, cut into ¼-inch-thick slices

1 small onion, cut into ¼-inch rings

1 large apple, thinly sliced

1 tablespoon cornstarch

1. Combine 1 cup apple juice, vinegar, caraway seeds and thyme in small bowl.

2. Sprinkle pork chops with salt and pepper. Heat oil in large nonstick skillet over medium-high heat. Add pork chops; cook 5 minutes or until lightly browned, turning once. Transfer to plate.

3. Place cabbage, fennel and onion in same skillet. Pour in apple juice mixture. Reduce heat to medium-low; cover and cook 15 minutes, stirring occasionally.

4. Return pork chops and any accumulated juices to skillet. Add apple; cover and cook 5 minutes or until pork chops are barely pink in center. Use slotted spoon to transfer pork, apple and vegetables to plate; keep warm.

5. Stir remaining ⅓ cup apple juice into cornstarch in small bowl until smooth. Add to skillet; cook and stir over medium heat until sauce boils and thickens. Serve over pork and vegetables.   *Makes 4 servings*

polenta lasagna

gluten-free I egg-free I nut-free I soy-free

4 1/4 cups water, divided

1 1/2 cups whole grain yellow cornmeal

4 teaspoons finely chopped fresh marjoram

1 tablespoon olive oil

1 pound fresh mushrooms, sliced

1 cup chopped leeks

1 clove garlic, minced

1/2 cup (2 ounces) shredded mozzarella cheese

2 tablespoons chopped fresh basil

1 tablespoon chopped fresh oregano

1/8 teaspoon black pepper

2 medium red bell peppers, chopped

1/4 cup freshly grated Parmesan cheese, divided

1. Bring 4 cups water to a boil in medium saucepan over high heat. Slowly add cornmeal, stirring constantly. Reduce heat to low; stir in marjoram. Simmer 15 to 20 minutes or until polenta thickens and pulls away from side of saucepan. Spread in ungreased 13×9-inch baking pan. Cover and chill about 1 hour or until firm.

2. Preheat oven to 350°F. Spray 11×7-inch baking dish with nonstick cooking spray.

3. Heat oil in medium nonstick skillet over medium heat. Add mushrooms, leeks and garlic; cook and stir 5 minutes or until leeks are crisp-tender. Stir in mozzarella, basil, oregano and black pepper.

4. Place bell peppers and remaining 1/4 cup water in food processor or blender; process until smooth.

5. Cut cold polenta into 12 squares; arrange 6 squares in bottom of prepared dish. Spread with half of bell pepper mixture, half of vegetable mixture and 2 tablespoons Parmesan. Repeat layers. Bake 20 minutes or until cheese is melted and polenta is golden brown.   *Makes 6 servings*

orange chicken stir-fry over quinoa

gluten-free | dairy-free | egg-free | nut-free

½ cup uncooked quinoa

1 cup water

2 tablespoons vegetable oil, divided

1 pound boneless skinless chicken breasts, cut into strips

1 cup fresh orange juice (2 to 3 oranges)

1 tablespoon gluten-free soy sauce

1 tablespoon cornstarch

2 tablespoons grated fresh ginger

¼ cup sliced green onion

1 cup thinly sliced carrots

6 ounces snow peas, trimmed

¼ teaspoon red pepper flakes (optional)

1. Place quinoa in fine-mesh strainer; rinse well under cold running water. Transfer to medium saucepan; add 1 cup water. Bring to a boil. Reduce heat to low; cover and simmer 12 to 15 minutes or until water is absorbed and quinoa is tender.

2. Meanwhile, heat 1 tablespoon oil in large skillet over medium-high heat. Add chicken; stir-fry 4 to 6 minutes or until cooked through. Remove and keep warm.

3. Stir orange juice and soy sauce into cornstarch in small bowl until smooth. Heat remaining 1 tablespoon oil in skillet. Add ginger and green onion; stir-fry 1 to 2 minutes. Add carrots and snow peas; stir-fry 4 to 5 minutes or until carrots are crisp-tender.

4. Return chicken to skillet; stir orange juice mixture and add to skillet. Bring to a boil. Reduce heat; simmer until slightly thickened. Serve over quinoa and sprinkle with red pepper flakes, if desired.

Makes 4 servings

turkey piccata

gluten-free | dairy-free | egg-free
nut-free | soy-free

2½ tablespoons rice flour

¼ teaspoon salt

¼ teaspoon black pepper

1 pound turkey breast, cut into strips

2 tablespoons olive oil

½ cup gluten-free chicken broth

Grated peel of 1 lemon

2 teaspoons lemon juice

2 cups cooked rice

2 tablespoons finely chopped parsley

Slow Cooker Directions

1. Combine rice flour, salt and pepper in resealable food storage bag. Add turkey strips and shake well to coat. Heat oil in large skillet over medium-high heat. Add turkey strips in single layer; cook 4 minutes or until browned. Arrange in single layer in slow cooker.

2. Pour broth into skillet, scraping up browned bits. Pour into slow cooker. Add lemon peel and juice. Cover; cook on LOW 2 hours. Serve over rice. Sprinkle with parsley.   *Makes 4 servings*

Tip: It's a shame to limit turkey to Thanksgiving Day. Try substituting turkey in your favorite chicken recipe; it is lean, flavorful and an excellent source of protein.

Sweets & Treats

allergy-free strawberry cake

gluten-free | dairy-free | egg-free | nut-free

1 package (15 ounces) gluten-free yellow cake mix

½ cup rice milk

½ cup dairy-free margarine

Prepared egg replacer equal to 3 eggs

2 teaspoons grated lemon peel

1 teaspoon vanilla

1 cup sliced strawberries

1 to 2 tablespoons powdered sugar

4 large strawberries, sliced (optional)

1. Preheat oven to 350°F. Spray 9-inch round cake pan with nonstick cooking spray.

2. Beat cake mix, rice milk, margarine, egg replacer, lemon peel and vanilla in large bowl with electric mixer at low speed 30 seconds. Beat 1 minute at medium speed. Add strawberries; beat 1 to 2 minutes or until strawberries are crushed. Spoon batter into prepared pan.

3. Bake 35 to 40 minutes or until cake is golden brown and firm to the touch. Cool in pan 10 minutes. Remove to wire rack; cool completely. Dust with powdered sugar and garnish with strawberry halves.

Makes 8 servings

chocolate sandwich cookies

 gluten-free | dairy-free | nut-free

¾ cup dairy-free margarine, divided
1 package (15 ounces) gluten-free chocolate cake mix
4 to 5 tablespoons vanilla rice milk, divided
1 egg
3 tablespoons unsweetened cocoa powder, divided
1 tablespoon tapioca flour
1½ cups powdered sugar
Marshmallow creme (optional)

1. Preheat oven to 350°F. Line cookie sheet with parchment paper. Melt ½ cup margarine in small saucepan over low heat.

2. Beat cake mix, melted margarine, 2 tablespoons rice milk, egg, 1 tablespoon cocoa and tapioca flour in large bowl with electric mixer at medium speed 1 minute or blended and dough comes together. Add additional 1 tablespoon rice milk, if needed. Shape level tablespoonfuls of dough into balls; place 1 inch apart on prepared cookie sheet.

3. Bake 10 minutes. (Cookies will puff up and be very delicate.) Cool on cookie sheet 10 minutes. Remove to wire rack; cool completely.

4. For chocolate filling, beat remaining ¼ cup margarine, 2 tablespoons cocoa, 2 tablespoons rice milk and powdered sugar in large bowl with electric mixer at high speed until light and fluffy.

5. Spread scant tablespoon chocolate filling or marshmallow creme on half of cookies; top with remaining cookies.

Makes 18 sandwich cookies

marble sheet cake

gluten-free I dairy-free I egg-free I nut-free

    9 teaspoons powdered egg replacer, divided
1⅔ cups plus 4 tablespoons water, divided
    1 package (15 ounces) gluten-free yellow cake mix
    1 cup (2 sticks) dairy-free margarine, softened, divided
    2 teaspoons vanilla
    1 package (15 ounces) gluten-free chocolate cake mix
        No-Butter Buttercream Frosting (page 271)
        Gluten-free sprinkles or other decorations

1. Preheat oven to 350°F. Spray 13×9-inch baking pan with nonstick cooking spray. Combine 4½ teaspoons powdered egg replacer and 2 tablespoons water in small bowl; mix well. Combine remaining 4½ teaspoons egg replacer and 2 tablespoons water in another small bowl; mix well.

2. Beat yellow cake mix, ½ cup dairy-free margarine, ⅔ cup water, one bowl of egg replacer and vanilla in large bowl with electric mixer at low speed 30 seconds or until combined. Beat at medium speed 2 minutes or until smooth.

3. Beat chocolate cake mix, remaining ½ cup dairy-free margarine, 1 cup water and remaining bowl of egg replacer in large bowl with electric mixer at low speed 30 seconds or until combined. Beat at medium speed 2 minutes or until smooth.

4. Spoon yellow cake batter and chocolate cake batter alternately into prepared pan. Swirl together in zigzag pattern with knife or spatula for marble effect.

5. Bake 40 to 50 minutes or until toothpick inserted into center comes out almost clean. Cool completely in pan on wire rack.

6. Meanwhile prepare No-Butter Buttercream Frosting. Frost and decorate cake as desired.   *Makes 16 servings*

no-butter buttercream frosting

 gluten-free | dairy-free | egg-free | nut-free

- ½ cup (1 stick) dairy-free margarine
- 2 teaspoons vanilla
- 4 cups powdered sugar
- 4 to 6 tablespoons soy creamer

1. Beat margarine in large bowl with electric mixer at medium speed until light and fluffy. Beat in vanilla.

2. Gradually beat in powdered sugar until well blended. Beat in soy creamer, 1 tablespoon at a time, until spreadable.

Orange No-Butter Buttercream Frosting: Reduce vanilla to 1 teaspoon and add juice of ½ orange. Adjust texture with additional powdered sugar or soy creamer as needed.

sunflower seed butter cookies

gluten-free | dairy-free | nut-free | soy-free

    1 cup creamy sunflower seed butter*
    1 cup sugar
    1 egg
    1 teaspoon vanilla
    ½ cup mini allergen-free chocolate chips

Do not use "natural" sunflower seed butter that separates.

1. Preheat oven to 350°F. Line cookie sheet with parchment paper.

2. Combine sunflower seed butter, sugar, egg and vanilla in medium bowl. Stir until smooth and combined. Fold in chocolate chips. Drop dough by tablespoonfuls onto prepared cookie sheet. Flatten cookies in crisscross pattern with fork.

3. Bake 10 to 12 minutes or until firm. *Do not overbake.* Cool on cookie sheet 2 minutes. Remove to wire rack; cool completely.

Makes about 12 cookies

cantaloupe sorbet

gluten-free | dairy-free | egg-free
nut-free | soy-free

    6 cups cubed fresh cantaloupe
    ⅓ cup light corn syrup
    3 tablespoons lime juice

1. Place cantaloupe in food processor; process until puréed. Add corn syrup and lime juice; process until combined. Transfer to medium bowl and refrigerate until cold.

2. Pour into ice cream maker; process according to manufacturer's directions.

Makes 4 cups

intense chocolate ice cream

gluten-free | dairy-free | egg-free
nut-free | soy-free

2 cups plain rice milk
¼ cup tapioca flour
¼ cup unsweetened cocoa powder
6 tablespoons granulated sugar
¼ teaspoon salt
⅓ cup allergen-free chocolate chips
½ teaspoon vanilla

1. Stir ½ cup rice milk, tapioca flour and cocoa in medium saucepan until smooth. Stir in remaining 1½ cups rice milk, sugar and salt. Cook over medium heat, stirring constantly, until mixture thickens to consistency of pudding. Remove from heat; stir in chocolate chips and vanilla until chocolate melts.

2. Transfer to medium bowl; cover and refrigerate 2 hours or until cold.

3. Pour chocolate mixture into ice cream maker; process according to manufacturer's directions. *Makes 4 servings*

cocoa raisin-chip cookies

 gluten-free | dairy-free

1 ½ cups Gluten-Free All-Purpose Flour Blend (page 5)*
¼ cup unsweetened cocoa powder
1 teaspoon baking powder
½ teaspoon salt
¼ teaspoon xanthan gum
1 cup packed brown sugar
½ cup granulated sugar
½ cup (1 stick) dairy-free margarine
½ cup shortening
2 eggs
1 teaspoon vanilla
1 ½ cups dairy-free semisweet chocolate chips
1 cup raisins
¾ cup chopped walnuts

Or use any all-purpose gluten-free flour blend that does not contain xanthan gum.

1. Preheat oven to 350°F. Line cookie sheets with parchment paper or lightly grease and dust with flour.

2. Combine flour blend, cocoa, baking powder, salt and xanthan gum in medium bowl. Beat brown sugar, granulated sugar, margarine and shortening in large bowl with electric mixer at medium speed until light and creamy. Add eggs, one at a time, beating well after each addition. Beat in vanilla. Add flour mixture; beat until well blended. Stir in chocolate chips, raisins and walnuts. Drop tablespoonfuls of dough onto prepared cookie sheets.

3. Bake 10 to 12 minutes or until set. Remove to wire racks; cool completely. *Makes about 4 dozen cookies*

dairy-free | egg-free | nut-free

Replace gluten-free flour blend with all-purpose flour and eggs with ½ cup silken tofu. Omit xanthan gum and walnuts. Proceed as directed.

maple-oatmeal cookies

dairy-free | egg-free | nut-free | soy-free

1 ½ cups old-fashioned oats

¾ cup all-purpose flour

½ teaspoon ground cinnamon

½ teaspoon baking soda

¼ teaspoon salt

½ cup dairy-free soy-free margarine

½ cup packed brown sugar

½ cup maple syrup

½ cup raisins

1. Preheat oven to 375°F. Line cookie sheets with parchment paper. Combine oats, flour, cinnamon, baking soda and salt in medium bowl.

2. Beat margarine, brown sugar and maple syrup in large bowl with electric mixer at medium speed 1 minute or until creamy. Gradually beat in flour mixture just until blended. Beat in raisins.

3. Drop batter by heaping tablespoonfuls 1 inch apart on prepared baking sheet. Flatten to ½ inch thick. Bake 13 to 16 minutes or until golden. Cool on cookie sheet 5 minutes. Remove to wire racks. Serve warm.

Makes about 2 dozen cookies

pink peppermint meringues

gluten-free | dairy-free | nut-free | soy-free

3 egg whites

⅛ teaspoon peppermint extract

5 drops red food coloring

½ cup superfine sugar*

6 peppermint candies, finely crushed

Or use ½ cup granulated sugar processed in food processor 1 minute until very fine.

1. Preheat oven to 200°F. Line cookie sheets with parchment paper.

2. Beat egg whites in medium bowl with electric mixer at medium-high speed 45 seconds or until frothy. Beat in peppermint extract and food coloring. Add sugar, 1 tablespoon at a time, while mixer is running. Beat until egg whites are stiff and glossy.

3. Drop batter by teaspoonfuls into 1-inch mounds on prepared cookie sheets; sprinkle evenly with crushed candies.

4. Bake 2 hours or until meringues are dry when tapped. Transfer parchment paper with meringues to wire racks to cool completely.

Makes about 6 dozen meringues